AYURVEDA AAHAR

(DIET/FOOD)

Indian Medical Science Series No. 104

AYURVEDA AAHAR
(DIET/FOOD)

by

Prof. Dr. P. H. Kulkarni

Former Dean

Faculty of Ayurvedic Medicine,

University of Pune.

Ayurveda Research Guide,

University of Pune

Director

Ayurveda Academy

and

Institute of Indian Medicine

Sri Satguru Publications

A Division of

Indian Books Centre

Delhi, India

Published by
Sri Satguru Publications,
Indological and Oriental Publishers
A Division of
Indian Books Centre
40/5, Shakti Nagar,
Delhi-110007
India

Email: ibcindia@ibcindia.com
Website: http://www.ibcindia.com/

First Edition; Pune 1998
Second Edition; Delhi, 2000

ISBN 81-7030-668-X

Published by Sunil Gupta for Sri Satguru Publications, a division of Indian Books Centre, 40/5, Shakti Nagar, Delhi-110007, India and printed at Chawla Offset Press, Delhi 110 052

Foreword

Study of Ayurveda is eternal. One can try to understand Ayurveda in one's life. It seems very difficult. Hence it is beneficial to study Ayurveda everyday, every life.

Whatever, I understood about Ayurveda, during last 44 years, I tried to write it. In this book salient features about various aspects of food are considered as described in Ayurvedic Treaties and recent research references are considered for benefit of interested persons.

Chikitsa (Treatment) of other diseases, Ayurveda soundarya (Beauty), Ayurveda Kitchen (cooking), Ayurvedic massage, Ashtang Ayurveda and such other books are in press.

Let Ayurveda help every body to be always happy !

P. H. Kulkarni

September 1998
Sanvito/Rome
Italy

Index

This book is
Dedicated to my
Students and patients of
Ayurveda Aahar (Diet/Food)
in all continents of the world

P. H. Kulkarni

PART ONE

PRINCIPLES OF AYURVEDA

Contents

1. UNIVERSAL NATURE OF AYURVED

Ayurveda is a science of life. Ayurveda accepts and asserts that every entity on this earth, living or non-living is produced by the five primordials or five pentads or Pancha Mahabhootas.

All living things in the world have **Jeevatmas** i.e. 'individual souls' or **' units souls'** which are part & parcel of cosmic i.e. **Paramatma** or the 'Almighty Himself'.

Every living things through its **'Jeevatma'** or Individual soul's is connected to every other living thing through **Paramatma** or 'Cosmic soul'.

Not only that, but even every thing, living or non-living is in connection directly or indirectly, with every other living or non-living in the universe either through five basic elements i.e. Panchamahabhootas or Five primordials or through cosmic soul or Parmatma.

Everything in this universe is acting and reacting with every other thing in it, in one way or other.

Ayurved holds that human being is a creation and epitome of mother nature according to 'Human body-Cosoms Principle' or 'Pind -Brahmand Nyaya'.

'Basic Principle of Ayurved' are founded on 'Three Basic Omnisubstances' i.e. **Trigunas,** on Five Primordials or Five Pentades i.e. Panchamahabhootas and also on Three basic elements or humors i.e. **Tridoshas.** The basic principles of Ayurveda are applicable to any and every human being on this earth.

Ayurveda imparted its profound knowledge to the world

without reservations or sacntions and also accepted new ideas from others with broad and open mind.

Naturally Ayurveda progressed speedily in depth and expanse and became the first most developed medical science in the world.

Even modern concept of 'Complimentary Medicine' was put forward hundreds of years before by one of the champion of Ayurved saying, 'Study of one science cannot give definite and perfect knowledge of the related subject. So to attain accuracy, competence and mastery in medical profession a physician should undergo comparative study of number of different medical disciplines.

2. UNIQUE FEATURES OF AYURVEDA

(1) Ayrveda is a well balanced medical science. It teaches how to maintain a perfect healthy condition. It is also describes the ways and means to prevent various diseases. Then it turns to the diagnosis and treatment of various diseases.

(2) Holistic approach, while treating a patient is a unique feature of Ayurveda. While diagnosing, the constitution, mental make up are also taken into account with the signs and symptoms of a disease. Disease may be the same, but the drugs vary according to the constitutuional and mental characteristics of the patient.

(3) Ayurveda is the first medical science in the world which knew th importance of mind in maintaining perfect health. Ayurveda also understood the vital role of mind as an aetiological factor in creation of a disease and at the same time it can be a useful means in curing a disease.

Ayurved determined the inseparable unity of mind and body.

(4) Ayurveda logically inferred the peculiar exceptional and twofold nature of mind. Ayurveda asserts that mind is Ubhayendriya i.e. it acts as a sense organ i.e. Dnyanendriya and Organ of function i.e. Karmendriya at the same time. It is a bridge between soul and physical body as well.

(5) Another unique finding of Ayrveda is that quality of mind as affected very greatly by nature of food you eat. Satva, Raja and Tama are the three qualities of mind and of the food as well. Food of satvika quality will boost up satvik nature of mind. Same is the case with Rajasik and Tamasik natures of food. Persons eating vegetarian diet in natural forms like fruits, milk, honey etc. are generally of satvik i.e. gentle nature. People eating non-vegetarian diet are of Rajasik nature i.e. of aggressive and arrogant nature. While people eating unhygienic, contaminated, non-nutricious, ill-preserved food and having addiction like alcohol, opium are of Tamasik nature i.e. they are ignorant and wayward.

(6) Ayurveda believes in the existence of spiritual dimension of human being. It states the principle of 'Jeevatma and Paramatma' and asserts further that Human soul, which is centre of vitality of human life, is part and parcel of Cosmic soul. As human soul which originates from and ends in cosmic soul at the time of birth and death respectively of a human being, it is fountain of tremendous energy which can be tapped and utilised by specific ways and means, as a preventive and curative instrument in medical therapeutics.

(7) Ayurveda is based on basic philosophy of its own.

It includes three important concepts.

(a) Concept of Three Basic Omnisubstances i.e. Trigunas viz. Satva, Raja and Tama which are a creative cause of five primordials or five pentads i.e. Panch Mahabhootas.

(b) Five Pentads i.e. Panchamahabhootas viz. Pruthvi (Earth), Aapa (Water), Agni (Energy or Fire), Vayu (Air) and Akasha (space). They are the causative factors or tridoshas i.e. three biological elements viz. Vat, Pitta and Kapha. Everything in this world is made up of five pentads. The variety of form, shape and quality is due to various percentages of the five pentads.

(c) Three biological elements i.e. Tridoshas, Human body, the diseases and the drugs, which are basically originated from five pentads have their biochemical base on tridoshas and their structures and actions i.e. anatomy and physiology is controlled by tridoshas i.e. three humors. This tripod base makes it easier to ascertain constitution i.e. Prakruti of a patient, to diagnose a disease and to select a suitable madicine for it. Also applying the tridosha theory hints of health can be given to the patient about correct diet, correct behaviour which will cut off aetiology of the disease (Nidan parivarjana) and speed up recovery without side effects. This tridosha theory is helpful also for minute differential diagnosis, prognosis and also for prevention of a disease.

(8) Local Abnormality i.e. Sthan Vaigunya is a peculier concept of Ayurveda. If the vitality and resistance of an organ or a tissue becomes weaken, there is every possibility of that organ or tissue to be diseased. The local abnormality may be structural or/and functional. When the increased

or vitiated tridoshas occupy this weak or debilitated organ or tissue, disease of'that particular organ or tissue becomes a certainty. But if the organ or tissue is normal in all respects the increased or visiated doshas cannot invade and occupy it and the organ successfully escapes the possibility of any disease.

(9) 'Agni Concept' of Ayurveda is also a unique feature of Ayurveda. Agni is a fire element and has digestive and metabolic power. If the agni becomes weaker the digestion and metabolic processes are disturbed. The incomplete and abnormal digestion and metabolism induce formation of a toxic substance called 'Aam' in the partially digested food. This aam infects the increased doshas and vitiate them into Saaṁ Doshas which are toxic in nature. These toxic saam doshas, being more virulent and more aggressive, increase the severity of the disease they produce. While treating any severe disease the aam element of the causative dosha is eliminated first by increasing the power of Agni to a normal functional level and then the treatment is directed to reduce the increased quantity of the related dosha.

(10) Panchakarma is another unique feature of Ayurveda. Vaman (Vomitting), Virechana (Purging), Basti (Enemata), Raktamoshana (Local or Systemic blood letting) and Nasya (to put medicated drug in nostrils) are the five procedures carried out and are important as well as essential part of Auyrvedic therapeutics.

Before each panchakarma, Snehan i.e. oiling or lubricating the intestinal tract with oil or ghee which are pure or medicated, Śwedan i.e. heating or fomenting the body to a point of sweating is carried out.

This typically specific mode of treatment is often used as a preventive as well as curative measure in Ayurvedic Therapeutics.

3. EVOLVEMENT OF LIFE

(A) According to Aurveda the causative factors behind the creation of the universe are as follows -

(1) Swabhav - It means natural property of a substance. To become an origin of the creation of the universe, through changes in the 'Three Basic Omni Substances' is natural property or Instinct of Prakruti. To go on changing, to show typical qualities, to create one thing from another is also nature of Prakruti.

(2) Eeshwar - It means Almighty. Brahma in Vedant philosphy, 'Purush' in Sankhya philosophy are similar to 'Eeshwar' in Vaisheshika philosophy. Paramatma is synonym for Eeshwar. According to Ayurveda 'Jeevatma' i.e. Vital Force or Pranashakti or Chaitanya in pure energy form in human being, is incarnation of Almighty. This Vital Force or Jeevatma keeps human being alive and active. When it leaves the body, human being stops living.

(3) Kaal - It means concept of Time. Creation, existence and destruction is intimately related to Time Factor. Various stages of growth e.g. Childhood, Youth, Oldage etc. various stages of digestion e.g. avasthapaka, vipak etc. stages of growth of tridoshas e.g. sanchaya (accumulation) prakopa (over growth) prasara (over flowing), are dependant on time factor.

(4) Yadruchcha - It means unknown cause. Any happening, for which definite 'cause and effect' rule is not applicable, is said to be due to unknown causal factor. An event or occurance taking place by chance, for which how and why, when and where get no reply. Creation of Universe is the model example of yadruchcha because no definite motive, clear reasoning or logical explanation of it can be given.

(5) Niyati - It means fate. It is exactly opposite of yadruchcha. Niyati or fate is controlled by the fruitful effects of good or bad deeds. Universe is created as a result of the collective fruits of actions of all individuals, getting mature.

(6) Parinaama - It means result, outcome or consequence. Creation of universe is supposed to be outcome or consequence of different combinations of Trigunas or Three Basic Omnisubstance, viz. 'Satva', Raja and Tama. The causative factors of 'Parinama' are svabhav, eeshwar, kaal, yadruchcha and niyati.

Eventhough the above six factors are said to be causative factors behind creation of universe except Eeshwar (God), the other five factors are the effects or expressions of Prakruti, whereas Eashwar i.e. omnipotent, omnipresent, self-created, self-dependant, birthless, deathless power form is a cause of changes in Prakruti. Purusha is synonym for Eeshwar.

(B) Indian Philosophies and Ayurveda

(1) Ayurveda like Vedant, Yog, Sankhya, Nyaya and Vaisheshik philosophies believes in the theory of Rebirth, which is controlled by one's own deeds and desires in one's past lives.

(2) Ayurveda respects the theories of creation of the universe and the origin of man as proposed by the above

philosophies, but believes in those which accept theory of rebirth.

(3) Charak, mentions the various accepted views from different philosophies, as given below :-

(a) The individual is represented by the soual principle as in Advait philosophy.

(b) The individual is composed of five basic elements (i.e. five pentads) and soul as proposed by Vaisheshik school of thought.

(c) Man is composed of the twenty four elements (viz. Prakruti, Mahat, Ahankar and five minute basic elements i.e. five tanmatras, which in combination of eight are called Ashta Prakruti + 16 Vikaras which include 11 Indriyaas - 5 dnyanendriyas, 5 karmendriyas and mind with 5 pentads i.e. 5 Mahabhootas) of Prakruti and Purush as proposed by Sankhya school.

(4) Ayurveda holds that all the non-living or inanimate objects in the universe, are created by combining in various ways the minute indivisible particles of earth, water, energy, air and space. So also, all living creatures from microbes to man originate from the combinations in various ways, of the same indivisible particles of the five primordials together with mind and unit souls.

(5) This creation process is the result of the fruits of actions i.e. Karmaphalas of all the individuals getting mature. The individuals enjoy the fruits of their actions (Karmaphal Theory) during the existence of the universe.

(6) When the fruits of actions of all the individuals are immature and are in abeyance, these minute indivisible particles start separating form one another, till they are

completely separated. This total process of destruction is called Pralaya.

(7) Ayurveda also believes in God, The Supreme Power. the Origin of Orgins.

(8) It can be seen that, while building up the science of Ayurveda by stalwarts like Charak, Sushruta, Vagbhata etc. all the currents of Indian Philosophy were tackled by them and after elaborate thinking, deep discussions and logical analysis, the selected principles befitting their line of thought and making up the missing lapses, were accepted irrespective of their origin.

(C) Sankhya Theory of Creation

(I) This theory was put forward by Mahamuni Kapil. The word Sankhya is composed of two Sanskrit words, 'Sam' means 'thoroghly' and the verb 'khya' means 'to know'. Thus 'Sankhya' means a philosophy, by which can understand thoroghly well, all the elements in the universe.

(II) Main elements taking part in the creation of Universe :-

(1) Purusha - Is Origin of all vitality. He is 'All-Knowing' principle and is without beginning or end. He is also Omnipresent, Eternal and having no qualities or properties. He is Seedless (Abeejadharmi) and without reproductive property (Aprasavadharmi) but is a catalyst. He is Unmanifest (Avyakta) and Inactive (Nishkreeya), without refuge and without organs or divisions. He does not act as a medium (Amadhyastha dharmi). In each living thing there is Unit Purush i.e. Jeevatma, Parabrahmha, Paramatma, Eeshwar are syonyms for Purusha.

(2) Prakruti - She is Omnipresent, without beginning (Anaadi) and without end (Anant). She is massive, inactive and without vitality. She is having properties or qualities (Saguna). She is in the form of seed and having reproductive and multiplying ability. She is the cause of the universe but herself is causeless. Prakruti, is common to everything (animate or inanimate) in this universe. Prakruti is trinity of Satva, Raja & Tama i.e. these three basic omnisubstances are part and parcel of Prakruti, in which they are in balanced state and are unmanifest.

(3) Mahat Principle - Is similar to Prakruti except that, it has intellect as its manifest quality. It arises from 'Prakruti'. It is in the universal form of knowledge. The knowledge of 'Purush' is reflected by Mahat. The desire and aversion, happiness and sorrow have their origin in Universal Intellect or Mahat principle. Satvik, Rajasik and Tamasik are the three forms of Mahat.

(4) Ahankara - It means 'Awareness of Self' and arises from Mahat principle. The Purush i.e. the 'Universal soul' identifies self with mind intellect in 'Ahankara stage'. The Trigunas classify Ahankara, into three types viz. (a) Satvik or Vaikarika Ahankara, (b) Rajsik or Taijasik Ahankara (c) Tamasik or Bhootadi Ahankara.

(III) Stages in creation of Universe :-

(A) First Stage : When "Prakruti and Purush' came together, due to catalystic property of Purush the normal balanced state of Trigunas in Prakruti (viz. Satva, Raja and Tama) got disturbed. Thereby the 'Raja' portion of the Prakruti became active. With the creative and stimulant effect of 'Rajoguna', the 'Satva-guna' in the Prakruti bloomed up and Mahat Principal having qualities of Satvaguna, viz. knowledge or intellect, light or brightness and minuteness, originated from Prakruti.

(B) Second Stage - First 'Satvaguna' in Mahat dominated then, secondly 'Rajoguna' and finally Tamoguna excelled in dominance. Then from 'Mahat' principle arose 'Ahankar' (awareness of self), having properties of Trigunas viz. Satva, Raja and Tama.

(c) Third Stage - As previously stated, Ahankar is of three types viz. Satvik, Rajasik, Tamasik.

(i) The Five Sense of hearing, touch, vision, taste, smell were produced predominantly by 'Satvik Ahankara' being incited by Rajasik Ahankara.

(ii) The Five subtle Organs of Action - Situated in the centres, controlling actions of speech, hands, feet, anus and sex organs (in male and female) and which themselves are controlled by 5 Vatdoshas viz. Prana, Udana, Vyaana, Samana and Apana components of the nervous system respectively, originated predominantly from 'Rajasik Ahankara.

(iii) Mind, which has both sensory and motor components (and so named as Ubhayendriya) originated from Satvik and Rajasik Ahankaras.

(iv) Five Tanmatras i.e. 'five minute basic elements' viz. Sound (Shabda), Touch (Sparsha), Appearance (Roop), Taste (Rasa) and Smell(Gandha) originated from Tamasika or Bhootadi Ahankara, being incited by Rajasik Ahankara.

(v) At the end of the third stage Subtle Body (Sookshma Shareera), which is composed of 5 Senses, 5 Motors Centres, 5 Pranas, Mind, Ahankara and Intellect i.e. Mahat Principle came into existence.

(D) Fourth Stage -

(i) Five Gross sense organs viz. Ears, Skin, Eyes, Tongue and Nose originated from five senses of hearing, touch , vision, taste and smell respecitvely.

(ii) Five Gross Motor Organs viz. larynx, hands, feet, anus and penis or vagina originated from the subtle organs, situated in the centres controlling working of speech, hands, feet, anus and sex organs respectively.

(iii) Five Primordials or Pentads viz. Space (Aakasha), Air (Vayu), Energy or Fire (Teja), water (Aap) and Earth (Pruthvi) originated from 5 Tanmatras i.e. 5 Minute Subtle Elements of Sound (Shabda) Touch (Sparsha), Appearance (Roop), Taste (Rasa) and Smell (Gandha) respectively.

(iv) The Gross Body (Sthool Shareer) which is composed of Subtle Body (including 18 components) together with 5 Basic Elements or Pentads was produced at the end of the fourth stage.

(E) Fifth Stage -

All the inanimates or non-living objects in this universe were created by variety of combinations in different proportions of the 5 Pentads i.e. Panchamahabhootas.

All the animates or living beings in this universe, from microbes to man, were created in this last stage by variety of combinations, in different proportions of 5 Pentads or Panchamahabhootas with mind and soul i.e. Individual Purusha Principle.

4. PANCHAMAHABHOOTAS (FIVE GREAT ELEMENTS)

(1) The Five Basic Elements or 5 Pentads or 5 primordials are gross in nature yet unmanifest and are derived from the mixture of Tama components of Five Subtle Basic Elements, (SBE) which are pure and minute and refered to in Ayurveda as Panch Tanmatras.

(2) All the inanimate objects in the universe and bodies of living creatures including man are composed of the five basic elements viz. (i) Space i.e. Aakasha, (ii) Air or Wind (i.e. Vayu), (iii) Energy (i.e. Teja), (iv) Water (i.e. Aap), (v) Earth (i.e. Pruthvi).

(3) Sequence of formation of 5 Pentads :-

(a) Subtle basic elements of sound (Shabda tanmatra) gives rise of Space Pentad i.e. Aakash Mahabhoot. (with the help of Tamasik Ahankar.) which has shabda as its peculiar quality.

(b) S. B. E. s of Sound and Touch (Shabda and Sparsh Tanmatras) together give rise to Air Pentad which has shabda, sparsha as its peculiar qualities.

(c) S. B.E. s of Sound, touch and Vision jointly give rise to Energy Pentad, having sound, touch and vision as its peculiar qualites.

(d) S. B. E. s of Sound, Touch, Vision and Taste jointly give rise to Water Pentad, which has sound, touch, vision, taste as its peculiar qualities.

(e) S.B.E.s of Sound, Touch, Vision, Taste and Smell jointly give rise to Earth Pentad, which has sound, touch, vision, taste & smell as its peculiar qualities.

Details of Five Pentads :-

(A) Space (Aakash)

(i) It is an omnipresent and 'all-pervading' element.

(ii) It serves as an abode to all the other four elements and all objects in the universe.

(iii) It is because of space that one can separate or differentiate variety of numerous objects, and also different parts of an object.

(iv) It is made up of 50% of S. B. E. of sound and 12.5% of other four S. B. E. s.

(v) Sound, oneness, limitless expanse (Vibhutva), Separateness (Pruthaktva), Intergration and Segregation (Sanyoga, Vibhaga), Convergence and Divergence (Ekatrita and Vibhaktata), Nonhindrance (Apratighatatva), Lightness, Smoothness, Softness, Inactivity, Clarity, Minuteness, Neither hot nor cold, No movement are the qualities of Space Pentad.

(vi) Sense of hearing is connected with it and its sense organ is ear.

(vii) Vacuum in the intestinal tract, blood vessels, lymphatics, intercelluar spaces and vacuum anywhere in the body is manifestation of Space Pentad.

(viii) Ether or Superfluid composed of matter and antimatter can be a modern concept of Space Pentad.

(ix) Relation to mind - Satvaguna of mind is dominated by Space.

(x) Relation to Taste - Bitter taste is dominated by Air and Space.

(xi) Relation to seasons - Shishir or Late winter is perdominated by Air and Space.

(xii) Relation Quality - Lightness is dominated by Energy, Space & Air, Softness is dominated by Water and Space.

(xiii) Relation to Pharmacological actions - Relieving of odema is due to Space & Air.

(xiv) Relation to Dosha - Vat dosha is constituted by Space and Air.

(xv) Space has no movement and no taste.

(B) Air or Wind (i.e. Vayu)

(i) Air contains Oxygen, which is vital for existence of all living creatures.

(ii) Wind is responsible for all the movement in the nature, such as movements of clouds, leaves etc.

(iii) It is in presence of Oxygen in air that fire can exhibit its action.

(iv) It exerts drying effect on other elements and objects.

(v) Air Pentad is composed of 50% of S. B. E. of Touch and 12.5% of each of other four S. B. E. s.

(vi) Its Special Senese is Touch and Special Organ is skin.

(vii) It controls all body activities, pulsations, and all gaseous components. Inspired Air, Expired Air and all functions of the body are the body entities, it manifests.

(viii) Various gases (Hydrogen, Oxygen, Carbonic acid gas, H_2S), smoke of various substances are its manifestations in diet and digestive tract.

(ix) 'Vat Dosha' is produced by combination of 'Space' and 'Air' pentads in excess.

(x) Asthi Dhatu (Bone tissue) and Expired Air are composed of Earth and Air.

(xi) Rajoguna of Mind is dominated by Air.

(xii) Tastes and Air Pentad :- Pungent taste is composed of Air and Energy Pentads. Bitter taste is composed of Air and Space pentads. Astringent Taste is composed of Air and Earth Pentads.

(xiii) Seasons and Air Pentad - Late Winter (Shishira) is dominated by Air + Space pentads. Spring (Vasanta) is dominated by Air and Earth Pentads. Summer (Greeshma) is dominated by Air and Energy Pentads.

(xiv) Body and Air Pentad - Air Pentad is predominant through various pharmacological actions in upper as well as lower parts of the body.

(xv) Properties of Air Pentad - Lightness, Roughness, Clarity, Minuteness (Atomic in nature), Neither hot nor cold, Movement is active and centrifugal (outward). Also it helps other pentads in Soothing, Stimulating , Oedema-relieving, Splitting and wound healing activities. Also it exerts Drying Effects on other pentads and objects.

(3) Energy or Fire (i.e. Agni or Teja) -

(i) The Sun and Fire are the main sources of energy in nature. The Sun maintain an equitable environmental temperature and gives light. Both are essential or Vital for survival of life.

(ii) Energy pentad is composed of 50% of S. B. E. of Vision plus 12.5% of each of other four S. B. E. S.

(iii) All the metabolic processes like ripening and decaying of fruits and leaves depend on Sun and Energy.

(iv) It causes evaporation of water and formation of clouds, which supply water to the earth.

(v) Pitta dosha carrying agni with its manifold activities in the body and body warmth and skin lusture are the manifestations of Energy Pentad in the body.

(vi) Properties of Energy - Lightness, Roughness, Sharpness, Clarity, Minuteness, Hotness, Dryness, Luminosity are its properties. Also it has active spread and high speed. its movement is in upward direction.

(vii) Its taste is Pungent (Katu), Slightly Sour (Kinchit Amla) and Salty (Lavana)

(viii) Its special sense is Vision and special sense organ is Eye.

(ix) It is present in the diet in spices e.g. pepper, ginger. asafoetida, garlic etc.

(x) Pittadosha composed of Energy and Water pentads, is its manifestation in the body.

(xi) Tissue (Dhatu) - Blood is predominated by Water & Energy. (Upadhatu) - Menses is predominantly Energy manifestation.

(xii) Waste Product - Urine is predominated by Energy & Water.

(xiii) Quality of Mind - is Satvik and Rajasik due to energy.

(xiv) Pharmacological Actions

Site - Upper and lower parts of body.

Digestive Juices - Water and Energy dominate.

Digestion - Energy dominates through Pittadosha.

Splitting - Air and Energy dominate.

(4) Water or Liquid (i.e. Aap)

(i) Water in nature is contained in the sea, lakes, wells, clouds and rain. It exerts a cooling effect on the environmental temperature. It is essential for sustaining life.

(ii) It is composed of 50% of S. B. E. of Taste (Rasa) with 12.5% of each of other four S. B. E. s.

(iii) Properties - Massiveness (Jadatva), Fluidity (Dravatva), Softness (Mrudutva), Inactiveness (Nishkriyatva), Slimmyness (Shlakshnatva), Coldness (Sheetatva), Largeness of Molecules (Sthoolatva), Viscidity (Pichchilatva), Wetness (Aardratva), Downward movement due to gravitational force.

(iv) Taste - Sweet (Madhura), Slightly Astringent (Kinchit Kashaya), Slightly Salty and Sour (Kinchit Lawan, Kinchit Amla).

(v) Its special sense is Taste and its special organ is Tongue.

(vi) Body fluids such as blood, lymph, pitta, urine, sweat, semen etc. and also fatty tissue, kapha, stool etc. are the manifestations of Water Pentad in the body.

(vii) Relation to Doshas - Pittadosha is composed of Water and Energy Pentads while Kaphadosha is composed of Earth and Water pentads.

(viii) Relation Doshas and Malas - Plassma (Rasa dhatu),

Nervine Tissue (Majjadhatu) and Semen (Sukradhatu) are predominantly composed of Water Pentad. Fatty Tissue (Meda dhatu) is composed of water and earth pentads. Blood (Rakta dhatu) is composed of Water and Energy pentads. Breast Milk (Upadhatu Stanya) and Sweat (Sweda mala) are mainly composed of Water pentad. Urine (mootramala) is composed mainly of Water and slightly of Energy pentads. Stool (Pureesh mala) has some water content

(ix) Relation to Mind - Satvaguna and Tamoguna of Mind are related to Water pentad.

(x) Relation of Tastes - Sweet Taste (Madhura Rasa) is produced by Water and Earth Pentads. Sour Taste (Amla rasa) is produced by Water and Energy pentads. Salty Taste is produced by Water and Energy pentads.

(xi) Relation to Pharmacological Actions -

Site - lower part of the body mainly.

Soothing and Stimulating - due to Air, Water and Earth pentads.

Digestive Juices - dominated by Water and energy pentads.

Nourishing - dominated by Water and Earth pentads.

Cooling - dominated only by Water pentad.

Producing Oedema - dominated by Earth and Water pentads.

Healing of Wounds - dominated by Earth, Water and Air pentads.

(5) Earth or Solids (Pruthvi) -

(i) Earth itself is predominantly solid in nature. Man builds his house with solids to take shelter and protect himself from strom, heat, cold and rain. Food e.g. rice and wheat, that we eat, is composed mainly of solids. The solids maintain life and stability in nature.

(ii) Earth is made up of 50% of S. B. E. of Smell (Gandha) and 12.5% of each of other four S. B. E. s.

(iii) Properties - Massiveness (Jadatva), Roughness (Kharatva), Hardness (Kathinya), Slowness (Mandya), Inactiveness (Nishkriyatva), Steadiness (Santhatva) Firmness (Dardhya), Clarity (Sparshatatva), Denseness (Ghanatva), Largeness or bulkyness (Vishalatva or Sthoolatva). It is neither hot nor cold (Sama Sheetoshnatva).

(iv) Its Movement is in downward direction.

(v) Its Taste is predominantly sweet and associated taste is slightly astringent.

(vi) Its Special Sense is Smell and Special Sense Organ is Nose.

(vii) All organs, all solid substances in the body e.g. nails, bones, tendons, teeth, muscles, skin, stool, hair, spinal cord etc. are predominated by Earth Pentad.

(viii) Solid substances in diet like rice, wheat, mineral salt, carrot, beet, shatavari are predominated by earth element.

(ix) Relation to Doshas - Kapha dosha is composed of Earth and Water pentads.

(x) Relation to Tissues (Dhatus) and waste products (Malas) Tissues-Muscular tissue (Mansa) is predominantly formed out of Earth Pentad. Fatty Tissue Meda dhatu is composed of Earth and Water Pentads. Bone Tissue (Asthidhatu) is composed of Earth and Air Pentads. Waste product stool (pureesh mala) is mainly composed of Earth Pentad.

(xi) Relation to Mind - Tamoguna of mind is predominated by Earth pentad.

(xii) Relation to Taste - Sweet Taste is dominated by Earth and Water pentads. Sour Taste is dominated by Earth and Energy pentads. Astriangent Taste is dominated by Earth and Air pentads.

(xiii) Relation to Seasons - In spring (Vasant) Air and Earth are predominant pentads. In Monsoon (Rain) (Varsha) Earth and Energy are predominant Pentads. In early winter (Hemant). Earth and Water are predominated pentads.

(xiv) Relation to Pharmacological actions -

Site - lower part of body.

Astringent action is dominated by Earth and Air pentads. Soothing and Stimulating actions are dominated by Air, Water and Earth pentads.

Nourishing action is dominated by Earth and Water pentads.

Producing Oedema - is dominated by Earth and Water pentads.

Healing of Wounds - is dominated by Earth, Water, and Air pentads.

Manifestations and Practical Utility of Pentad Theory :

(1) The human body is composed of earth, water, energy, air and space i.e. five basic elements or pancha mahabhoots. In the foetal growth Space (Aakash) element provides room to grow, Air (Vayu) element brings about cell division, Energy (Agni) promotes digestion and metabolism, Water (Aap) maintain fluid balance, Earth (Pruthvi) provides food to grow and keep cell mass together.

(2) Food, which nourishes the body, is also derived from the same five basic elements of which body is composed. These five basic elements in the food are digested by their respective enzymes (bhootagnis) in the body and after assimilation replace the respective worn out elements, in the various tissues and organs of the body. After death, the body decomposes and merges with the same five basic elements.

(3) Therapeutic measures used externally, with this 'pentad concept' can be demonstrated as -

(a) Maintenance of proper Space by keeping airways patent by suction.

(b) Giving oxygen i.e. 'Air' for anoxia.

(c) Application of heat energy by fomentation.

(d) Giving fluids i.e. Water in dehydration.

(e) Advising high calorie nourishing diet, providing Earth element for the undernourished and underweight.

(4) Food stuffs providing five basic elements.

(a) Rice and Wheat predominate in Earth element.

(b) Milk and Fruit juices predominated in Water

element.

(c) Spices which stimulate various enzymes predominate in Energy (Agni) element.

(d) Pulses predominated in the Air element and so produce gases.

(e) Popcorn cotains much more space than the corn from which it is derived.

Selection of drugs according to 5 Pentad Theory

(a) If the digestive power is weak, one should use spices which are rich in Energy element.

(b) If patient suffering from oedema one should avoid salt, as it's predominant element is Water.

(c) If patient is suffering from burning sensation he should be given grapes or watermelons, which have a cooling effect due to Water element.

(d) When an abscess suppurates and fluctuates caustic like sodium carbonate, which contain Energy and Air elements, should be applied.

(e) If healing or tonic effect is required drugs like Glycerrihza or Shatavari, predominated in Earth and Water element are given.

(f) Diets and drugs when taken, digested and assimilated in the body, increase the similar qualities and elements in the body e.g. Underweight person is given substances with sweet taste like rice, wheat, ghee etc. and drugs predominant in earth and water element like Shatavari and Vidari Kanda.

(g) On the other hand substances with opposite

properties antagonise the increased elements in the body and help to maintain a balanced state e.g. if a person has fever drugs like Musta and Lotus, which predominantly have cooling effect of Water element are given to reduce temperature produced by Energy element. If a person has a good deal of phlegm produced by predominance of Earth and Water elements, drugs which are bitter and pungent in taste like Pepper, Ringni, Dorli and Pushkarmool are given, as these drugs predominantly contain Energy and Air elements.

5. TRIGUNAS (OMNISUBSTANCES)

A) The tributes, which are causative factors of creation of Universe and which are omnipresent are called Master Tributes (Mahagunas) or Master Substances (Parama-Padarthas) or Omnisubstances (i.e. Trigunas) Viz. Satva, Raja & Tama. Prakruti represents a balanced state of Satva, Raja and Tama.

B) Properties or Qualities of the Trigunas :-

i) Satva - is Light, Luminous, Joyous & Extends Love & Affection. Though mind it unfolds Urnestness, Softness, Modesty, Satisfaction, Faith, Forgiveness, Kindness, Self Control knowledge & Happiness.

ii) Raja - is Mobile, stimulant, Endevour, Activeness, Negative & Saddening qualities like Hatred, Deception, Malice, Criticism, Pride, greed, egoism, conceit anger etc. are the expression of Rajoguna.

iii) Tama - Obstruction suppression and Resistance to

the qualities of Satvaguna, convering up of light and knowledge, Idleness, inactivity, Controversy, Fear, Atheism, Deceit, Mean-Mindness, Miserly nature, Ignorance, Blockheadedness etc. are the qualities of tama.

C) Mutual Relationship of Trigunas.

Satva-Raja-Tama qualities always exist together, depend on one another and try to dominate one another, eventhough they have opposite qualities, very interesting example of Oil lamp is given as an explanation. Here the cotton wick, Oil lamp and Fire having Opposite qualities are responsible for the light of the flame, when they work in co-ordination with one another. Satva enlighten Raja and Tama, Raja stimulates Satva and Tama and Tama Masks Satva and Raja.

D) Role of Omnisubstances i.e. Trigunas in the Creation of Universe.

Prakruti is Trinity of Satva, Raja, & Tama which are dorment, when they are in balanced state. When Purusha and Prakruti join each other the trigunas go out of balance and are excited to a great extent. Here Rajoguna due to its action and motion excites the creativity of Prakruti, in the presence of Purusha. It then activates the properties of knowledge, Light and Minuteness then give rise to Intellect i.e. Mahana. Then to counteract the aggravated Satvaguna, Tamoguna is promoted by Rajoguna, which reduces properties of satvaguna. Due to increased properties of Tama Viz. Affinity, Heaviness and staticity Ego (i.e. Ahamkara) becomes manifested by Intellect i.e. Mahana. Again due to the influence of Rajoguna Ahamkara (i.e. Ego) is subdivided into Satvika Ahamkara (dominated by Satvaguna) and Tamasika Ahamkara (dominated by

Tamoguna).

The Sense-Organs are derived from Satvik or Vaikarika Ahamkara. (Ears, Skin, Eyes, tongue and nose are sense organs.)

The Organs of Actions, situated in the brain centres which control speech, hands, feet, anus and sex organs and which are contolled by prana, Udana, Samana, Vyana and Apana are derived predominantly from Rajasika or Taijasika, Ahamkara.

Tanmatras or Basic Subtle Substances (Viz. Shabda, or sound, Sparsh or touch, Roopa or appearance, Rasa or taste, Gandha or smell and Panchamahabhootas or Gross Basic Elements (Viz. Space, Air, Energy, Water and Earth) are derived from Tamasika or Bhootadi Ahamkara.

All the living (animate) and nonliving (inanimate) objects are derived from Panchamahabhootas.

E) Mental Constitutions Acording to Trigunas.

i) Tamobhooyishta (Tamoguna Dominated Mentality)

a) Less intelligent

b) Depressed & Frustrated.

c) Lazy and Inactive

d) Less Mental Stamina.

e) Day-Sleepers

f) Indulged in Eating, Drinking, Sleeping and Sex

g) Greedy and Selfish

h) Unbalanced, Restless & Irritable.

i) Id dominated over Ego & Super-Ego.

ii) Rajobhuyista (Rajoguna-Dominated-Mentality)

A) Egoistic & Proud

B) Ambitious and Dominating.

C) Loguacious; Boasting

D) Hard working but no planning & direction

E) Emotions like anger, jealousy dominate over sentimental

F) Are good friends or bitter enemies.

G) Limited Self-Control.

H) Intelligent, Militant, Activist, Risk-Mongers & Extremist.

I) Id dominates over Ego & Super-ego

J) Medium Sleep (6-7 hrs.)

iii) Satvabhuyista (Satvaguna-Dominated-Mentality)

a) Steady & Pure Mind

b) Religious, Truthful & Righteous.

c) Good Manners & Character

d) Good Self-Control & Balance

e) Exceptional Mental stamina

f) Less sleep is enough (5hrs)

g) Respect & Honour Elders

h) Mature & Logical Thinkers.

i) Always engaged in improving Knowledge Proficiency & Skill.

j) They have Kind, Forgiving & Helping Nature.

k) Are constructive in thoughts & Actions.

ii) Super-ego dominates Id and Ego.

F) Trigunateeta & Purushottama.

i) Trigunateeta - It means he, who has mastered all the Mental processes going beyond trigunas. He has absolutely, no desires, no aversion, no emotions & no attachments, no expectations & no fears. He renouces all wordly pleasures.

E) ii) Purushottama - A Person having all the qualities of head and heart of Trigunateet together with pure Satvik Personality. In him, complete and full detachment of trigunateet happily combines with friendly, helpful and social nature. He places service before self and only lives for betterment of the Society. Shreekrishna is ideal example of purushottama.

D)Diet & Trigunas :-

Diet is the source of supply of Satva, Raja & Tama particles to Brain Cells. Diet like milk, fruits, butter & ghee provides Satvika particles. Pungent, Sour and Hot food items are rich in Raja Particles. Stale and Putrified food is rich in Tama Particles.

6. TIRDOSHA
(THREE ENERGIES/HUMORS)

It attributes, functions, formation, apperance & sub-types

Tridosha Concept

(a) Tridoshas or three humors are the three biological elements, which constitute the structural and functional units of all the living cells, tissues, organs and the body as a whole.

(b) Vaṭ, Pitta Kapha are the three doshas, which result from combinations of the atoms of four elements namely earth, water, air and energy and which exit in the form of molecules. These molecules form the basic constituents, from the biological union of which life originates and organism grows and matures.

(c) One molecule each of Vata, Pitta and Kapha is the minimum requirement for the begining of life in the most primitive form. Vata, Pitta and Kapha molecules are conventionally described as Doshas in Ayurvedic texts, irrespective of whether they function as dhatus, doshas, or malas.

Tridhatus - The molecules of Vata, Pitta and Kapha or their combinations, which are biologically active are termed as Tridhatus and represent tissues at molecular level e.g. the aminoacids i.e. molecules of Kapha-dhatu or Kaphadosha, combine with each other to form protein molecule, which is bigger molecule of kapha dhatu. Similarly Pitta molecules combine to form several enzymes and hormones, which constitute bigger molecules of pitta dhatu.

Tirdoshas - The same three biological elements are termed as Doshas when (1) their number is incerased i.e. doshvruddhi, (2) their number is decreased i.e. doshakshaya and (3) their quality is vitiated i.e. doshdushti. In these three states the three biological elements disturb the structure and function of the body and give rise to disease.

Trimalas - When molecules of Vata, Pitta and Kapha are further broken down or altered qualitatively to such an extent that their reversal to original state is impossible, they are termed as Trimalas, (in molecular state) as they cannot be utilised by the body anymore. Urea moleule represents Kaphamala molecule, Stercobilin and Urobilin represent pittamala molecules and carbondioxide and Ammonia represent molecules of Vatmala.

Formation

The three doshas namely Vata, Pitta and Kapha originate from the 5 Basic Elements i.e. earth, water, energy, air and space, which constitute the entire, universe. The biological combination of atoms of earth and water gives rises to Kapha molecules, that of atoms of water and energy to pitta molecules and that of atoms of air and space to Vata molecules.

The food we take, is composed of proteins, fats, carbohydrates, vitamins, minerals and water according to modern medicine. After digestion these components of food are divided into aminoacids, sugar, fatty acids, glycerol etc.

These basic structural molecules are classified by Ayurvedic scientists into Kapha, Pitta and Vata categories. They constitute a major portion of the rasadhatu i.e. body fluids. Apart from this Rasadhatu also consists of Kapha, Pitta & Vat molecules, which are derived from the cells of tissues and organs e.g. various enzymes, hormones, serum albumin etc.

Attributes & Functions

Though present throughout the body, Vata in general dominates the region below the umbilicus, Pitta between umbilicus and heart and Kapha above the diaphragm.

(a) Kapha Attributes - Kapha molecules are heavy, stable, smooth, soft, viscous, slimmy and moist. They are cold to touch, white in color and predominantly have a sweet and slightly salty taste. Beacuse of their centripetal movement, viscous and slimmy nature, they tend to adhere to each other, form bigger molecules and exist in gross form and give compactness to the body.

Functions :-

(1) Kapha constitutes the main body mass and is responsible for its shape and form.

(2) Kapha molecules in the bones predominate in the earth element and because of their heavy and stable qualities are responsible for strength, stability and firmness of the body.

(3) The water (fluid) component of Kapha is responsible for the formation and maintenance of bodyfluids in intracellular, interstitial and intravascular spaces.

(4) The interstitial fluid, which is composed of Kapha molecules, helps to prevent friction between the two cells and also acts as a 'fluid medium' through which cells get their nourishment.

(5) The body nutirents belong predominantly to the Kapha element. So Kapha naturally is responsible for all the anabolic processes including growth and development of the body and healing of wounds.

(6) Kapha molecules in the muscles give strength to the body, those in fatty tissue give form to it and those in semen are responsible for fertility.

(7) The brain and nervous tissues like other tissues predominantly contain Kapha molecules and are precursors of zeal, knowledge, memory, magnanimity, absence of greed and forgiveness, in short qualities of Satvik nature.

(b) Pitta Attributes - Pitta represents energy, heat or fire in the body. The energy component of pitta is ative principle wheras water component of it acts as a vehicle. The physical and biological properties of pitta represents the combination of properties of energy and water elements. Pitta is hot, light, clear, slightly viscous and has a penetrating Power. It is liquid in consistency and hence is mobile. It is pungent and sour in taste and has a strong and foul smell. If energy element is dominant it tends to move upwards whereas if liquid element is dominant it tends to move downwards.

Functions -

(1) Pitta increase the catabolic processes every where in the body i.e. break the bigger kapha molecules into smaller ones and also increases the motion of vata molecules.

(2) It increases heat production and body temperature.

(3) It increases appetite and thirst.

(4) Pitta maintains colour, complexion and lusture of skin. It renders the skin soft and thin.

(5) Since the eye, sense organ of vision is derived from energy element, pitta maintains the vision intact.

(6) The process of digestion continues in the gastrointestinal tract and in the tissues by means of various digestive and tissue enzymes designated collectively as pitta.

(7) Activities in the Central Nervous System, mind and intellect depend on pitta. By increasing the metabolism of brain it improves the mental activities.

(8) Qualities of both satvik and rajsik nature e.g. emotions like joy, fear, anger and courage, depend on the action of pitta.

(c) Vat Attributes Vat molecules are light, minute, clear rough and dry. They are mobile and move in all directions and spread quikly throughout the body. Its action is interrmittent. According to medicine, which deals with properties of all substances in relation to warm blooded human beings, vat is cold in nature. (According to physics air i.e. Vat is neither cold nor hot). Because of its minute nature it cannot be visualized in any form in the body, but its presence can be proved by its actions.

Functions -

Biological Functions

(1) It controls the movements of molecules, cells as well as the body and so is responsible for the organisation of all the tissues in the body.

(2) By bringing together kapha molecules and cells, it helps in regeneration and conjugation of tissues.

(3) It gives shape and form to embryo.

(4) It exerts drying effect on the body as well as as on pitta and kapha doshas.

(5) By stimulating movement and activity it increases the catabolism of the body.

(6) By controlling the speed of action, it controls the metabolic processes in the body.

(7) Vat is leader among the three doshas as it controls the movements and actions of pitta, kapḥa, all the body tissues and waste products in the body.

(8) It is responsible for origin, maintenance and destruction of life, strength, integrity and life itself depends on vayu or vat.

Nervous System related functions :

(9) It controls the actions of the prefrontal lobe, motor cortex and spinal cord and is responsible for smooth and co-ordinated movements.

(10) It carries all the sensory impulses to their centres and maintains the effeciency of sense organs.

(11) Sound and touch senses together with their sense organs, originate from Vat.

(12) It controls speech and speech centre. Also it controls respiratory centre and respiratory movements.

Mind and Intellect related functions :

(13) It is controller of mind and mental processes.

(14) It facilitates the normal functioning of the intellect.

Sites and Subtypes of Tridoshas

Kapha (Five varieties)

(1) Kledak - (a) This is present in the stomach and the intestines and is represented by mucus secretion there. (b) It is stickly, viscid, cold and slightly sweet. (c) It moistens the food and splits it into smaller parts and helps digestion of food. (d) It supports kapha elements present throughout the body.

(2) Avalambak - (a) This is present in the chest and is represented by kapha molecules present in the myocardium, alveoli, the pleural and pericardial fluids, the mucus secretions in the respiratory tract and the interstitial fluids in the lungs, hearts and mediastinum. (b) It supports and gives strength to the heart, lungs, bony cage and other sites. (c) It prevents friction and provides nutrition to the related parts. (d) By supporting circulation and respiration it supports whole body.

(3) Bodhak - (a) It is present in the oral cavity and throat and represented by saliva. (b) It helps in the appreciation of taste by the tongue. It does so by bringing the moistened and broken up food particles in close contact with the taste buds. (c) It helps in digestion of carbohydrates.

(4) Tarpak - (a) It is situated in the cranial cavity and is represented by kapha molecules of the brain, cerebrospinal fluid and interstitial fluid in the brain. (b) It supports functions of the brain including motor and sensory centres and maintain its nutrition.

(5) Shleshak - It is represented by synovial fluid in the joints. It provides nutrition to the bone-ends and prevent their friction during joint movements.

Pitta (Five varieties)

(1) Pachak Pitta - (a) It is present in the gastro-intestinal tract and is represented by all the enzymes secreted by gastro intestinal tract from Ptylin in saliva to the exzymes in the succus entericus. (b) It digests the food and then separates it into the 'Sara' i.e. useful portion and 'Kitta' i.e. waste product. (c) It supplements other types of pitta.

(2) Ranjak Pitta - (a) It is mainly in the liver, spleen, stomach and small intestine and is represented by bile, intrinsic factors in food and the enzymes in bone marrow. (b) Its function is synthesis of haemoglobin and imparting red colour to blood.

(3) Sadhak Pitta - (a) Brain is the main site of it and is represented by the cellular enzymes in the nerve cells. (b) By scanning the information and thought procresses, it maintains the normal functions of mind, ego and intellect. (c) It helps a person to have his desires fulfilled by maintaining proper mental activity.

(4) Alochak Pitta - (a) It is situated in eyes and is represented by the enzymes in the rods and cones in the retina. (b) Its function is perception of light.

(5) Bhrajak Pitta - (a) Its main site is skin. (b) It keeps the skin warm and is responsible for its normal complexion and luster. (c) It also helps in absorption and digestion of medicaments applied externally to skin.

Vat (Five varieties)

(1) Prana Vayu - (a) It is synonymous with life and is represented by the functional units of respiratory centre, sense and motor organs, mind, intellect and conscience. (b) It maintains life and life processes by supplying oxygen. (c) It supports the function of heart. (d) It supports and maintains the efficiency of the sensory and motor organs, the mind and intellect. (e) Inspiration, deglutition, sneezing and expectoration are controlled by it. (f) It is responsible for the rhythm and contractibility of the heart.

(2) Udan Vayu - (a) It controls speech and speech centre. (b) Diaphragm, chest, lungs, pharynx and nose are seats of action of it. (c) It maintains colour, complexion and strength by getting rid of gaseous waste products during expiration. (d) It maintains optimum zeal, effort and memory.

(3) Vyan Vayu - (a) It is present in the whole body including heart. (b) It is represented by the functional units in the spinal and higher centres i.e. all sensory and motor nerves, reflex arcs, motor centres and autonomic centres controlling circulation, sweat, secretion and capillary permeability. (c) Its high speed is seen during the transmission of nerve impulses. (d) All the voluntary and involuntary body body movements are controlled by it including reflex actions, (e) It controls circulation, sweat secretion and perfusion of tissue fluids through autonomic nervous system.

(4) Samana Vayu - (a) It is situated in the gastro intestinal tract from stomach to colon and is represented by the functional unit of autonomic nerous system, which controls peristaltic movement of stomach and intestines. (b) It helps reception of food by stomach and intestines and then the mechanical splitting of the food bolus into smaller parts so that pachak pitta i.e. digestive enzymes can act on the food in a more efficient manner. (c) It differentiates digested food into 'Sara' and 'Kitta' and then helps sara i.e. useful part to get absorbed and kitta i.e. waste products to be propulsed further into the colon.

(5) Apana Vayu - (a) Its sites are the pelvis, bladder, uterus, penis, thighs, testes, abdominal muscles pelvic colon and anus. (b) It is represented by the unit of lumbosacral autonomic system. (c) It controls the ejaculation of semen, expulsion of menstrual discharge, delivery of the foetus, defaecation and micturition.

Peculiarties of Tridoshas

(1) they are the physiological or functional units of the body and are active from birth to death. (2) They are not constant but keep on fluctuating from time to time. (3) Kapha dominates in children, in winter and spring seasons and its period of maximum activity is from 6 a.m. to 10 a.m. & from 6 p.m. to 10 p.m. and for sometime after meals. (4) Pitta dominates in adults, in monsoon and autumn seasons, and its period of maximum activity is from 10 a.m. to 2 p.m. and from 10 p.m. to 2 a.m. It dominates during digestion. (5) Vat dominates in old, in greeshma and varsha seasons. Its period of maximum activity is between 2 p.m. to 6 p.m. and between 2 a.m. to 6 a.m. It dominates after the digestion is over.

Influence of Daily Habits on Dosha

Diet	Vata	Pitta	Kapha
	lentils pulses	mustard	sesame, wheat, puffed rice
Vegetables	leafy vegetables onion	pods, (legumes) climbers drumsticks yam	lotus stalk
Fruit	watermelon	citrus fruits	dates, coconut, sugarcane

Meat		goat, sheep	meat of animals from marshy regions
Oil		sesame oil	ghee, butter
Alcohol			All types of alcohol
Dietary habits	irregular inadequate food	fasting	overeating excessive water drinking
Emotions	worry	anger, fear, sorrow	apathy
Exercise	excess activity swimming carrying heavy loads	less activity lack of exercise	laziness
Sleep	keeping awake	less sleep	excess sleep sleep in day time
Age	old	youth	childhood

■■■

7. SAPTADHATU (SEVEN TISSUES)

(1) RASA-DHATU

1. NAME : RASA - moving day and night
2. SITE : Heart, Rasavaha Srotasa
3. CONVERSION : From Ahara Rasa by Rasadhatwagni (PARINITI) (UTPATTI)
4. TIME : One day from taking food
5. NATURE : Sthayee (Native), Poshaka (Nutrient), Soumya, Snigdha (Oily), Sheeta (Cold), Guru (heavy), Sookshma (Subtle), Shweta (White).
6. SAAR : Twaksara (best skin), Suprasanna (happy), Mrudu (soft skins hairs) Twak-Roma.
7. QUANTITY : Nine Anjalee (Fistfuls) (Ahara)
8. FUNCTION : Preenava, (Udaka-Karma) (supply , nutrition + water). In old age less.
9. UPADHATU : Raja (manstrual fluid), Stanya (Breast milk)
10. MALA : Kapha.

(2) RAKTA DHATU

1. NAME : Rakta, Rudhira, Asruk, Lohita, Asra, Khataja, Shonitam

2.	SITE	: Yakrut (Liver), Pleeha (Spleen), Raktavaha Dhamani (Blood Vessel), Sira (veins), Raktavaha Srotasa (Blood Channels), Raktashaya (Raktadhara) (Blood Reservoir), AnuAsthi (Small Bones), Raktadhara Kala (Inner side) (Microscopic)
3.	CONVERSION	: From Rasa (best part)
	(PARINATI)	By Rakta dhatu agni
	UTPATTI	: Rakta Dhara Kala.
4.	TIME	: 3rd day, Sushrut 5, Parashar 3.
5.	NATURE	: Bright and Red Colour, Visra gandha, (Prithvi), Dravata (jala), Raktavarna (Teja), Spandan - (Vayu) Laghu- (Akasha), Panchabhoutika) Madhur, Lavana, Snigdha, Guru, Chala.
6.	SAAR	: Ear , Eyes, Face, lips, nose, palm, soles, are snighda (Oily), red, lusture cannot tolerate hot, pain (klesha)
7.	QUANTITY	: Eight Anjali
8.	FUNCTION	: Life (Jeevana), (Pranadharana), Colour of body, Dhatu poshan, Strength, Happiness, Sparshadnyana, Mamsa-poshaka (nutrition).
9.	UPADHATU	: Sthoola Snayu (Large muscles), Kandara, Tensions. Sira (veins)
10.	MALA	: Pitta

(3) MAMSA-DHATU

1. NAME	: Mamsa, Pishitam, Palalam, Kravyam, Amisasm.
2. SITE	: Under skin, around bones and organs, Mamsavaha Srotasa. (Muscle Channel)
3. CONVERSION (PARINITI) (UTPATTI)	: From Rakta - Mamsa dhatuagni, Mamsadhara kala
4. TIME	: 4th (S-10) (P-5)
5. NATURE	: Snigdha - oily, Sthira - Static, Ghana - solid, Shlakshna, Raktavarna, Parthiva.
6. SAAR	: Temporal, forehead, Occipital joint, eyes, chin, neck, shoulders, chest, hands, feet are heavily strong, surrounded by Mamsa, kind, intelligent, strong, healthy, happy, long life.
7. QUANTITY	: Cannot be determined.
8. FUNCTION	: Lepa - surround body and organs = cover, strength to body.
9. UPADHATU	: Vasa, Twak, Vasa is oil, Mamsa, Vapa is Moola, Snigdha (Oily), Vartika, fat globules, Vasa 3 Anjali - Charaka.
10. MALA	: Karna (ears), Nasa (Nose), Roma (Skin Pores), excretions.

(4) MEDA DHATU

1.	NAME	: Meda, Sneha, Twaka, dhatu.
2.	SITE	: All body, abdomen, Medodharakala, Medovaha Srotasa, Moola, Vrukka (Kidney), Vapavah, Kati (Pelvis)
3.	CONVERSION (PARINITI) UTPATTI	: From best part of mamsa.
4.	TIME	: 5th day (15)
5.	NATURE	: Atisnigdha (Oily), Guru (heavy), Sthoola (Large), Picchila (Sticky), Mrudu (Soft), Sandra, Varna-Shweta (White Colour), Prithvi, Jalabhooyishtha dhatu (Earth+Water).
6.	SAAR	: Varna (Colour), Swara (Voice), Netra (eyes), Kesha (hairs), Loma, Nakha (Nails), Danta (Teeth), Oshtha (Lips), Mootra (Urines), Purishna (Faeces), Sweda (Sweat), Sneh is present Sukumar - Rujuswabhava, happy, Vitta, Brihat Sharia, Ayasa - Asaishnu (Cannot tolerate)
7.	QUANTITY	: 2 Anjali
8.	FUNCTION	: Snehana (oleation) Sharira- drudhata. (Body Strength)
9.	UPADHATU	: Snayu
10.	MALA	: Sweda (Sweat), Drava (Liquid), Snigdha (Oily), Yellowsih, Vistra -

	going out of Bahya Twacha (Skin), To give softness to Kesha, Twak (Hair Skin).
	If Swedakshaya (Less Sweat) - falling of hairs, erect roma, skin cracking.

(5) ASTHI DHATU

1. NAME	: Asthi, Hadum, Kulyani, Kikasa, (Atharwaveda)
2. SITE	: Inside Mamsa, Meda. Asthivaha Srotasa.
3. CONVERSION (PARINATI) UTPATTI	: From best portion of Meda, Poshana - Pruthvi, Teja, Vayu + Shleshma = Meda (pariniti)
4. TIME	: 5 (20 days)
5. NATURE	: Hardest, strong, white coloured, Porous, (Pruthvi + Anila)
6. SAAR	: Large head, Large shoulders, strong Danta (Teeth), Strong Asthi (Bones), Strong Nakha (Nails).
7. QUANTITY	: No.
8. FUNCTION	: Dharana - Support. Movements-with Sandhi (Joints).
9. UPADHATU	: Danta (Sharangdhar)
10. MALA	: Nakha, Roma (Nails, Hairs).

(6) MAJJA DHATU

1. NAME	: MAJJA (Snigdha dhatu in Asthi)

2. SITE : Inside bones, Majjavaha Srotasa
3. CONVERSION : From best part of Asthi.
   (PARINATI) UTPATTI
4. TIME : Sixth day, 25 days.
5. NATURE : Atisnigdha, pichchila (Extreme oily Stickey)
6. SAAR : Soft body, slender body, strong oily voice, Joints are Sthoola (Round), Have long life, Learned, Rich, Knowledgeable
7. QUANTITY : One Anjali, 1/2 Anjali in skull
8. FUNCTION : Sneha (Oleation), Bala (Strength), Shukra pushti (Nutrition of Shukra).
9. UPADHATU :
10. MALA : Akshi Vit (eye thick secretions), Twak Sneha (Skin oil)

(7) SHUKRA - DHATU

1. NAME : Shukra, Teja, Reta, Beeja, Veerya, Indriyam.
2. SITE : All body (like ghee in milk) (Juice in Sugar cane), Shukravaha Srotasa, Vrushana (Scrotum), Jananendriya (Reproductive organ), Stana (Breast), Shukradhara Kala
3. CONVERSION : From all dhatus.
   (PARINATI) UTPATTI

4. TIME : 30 Days (16 yrs to 30 years)

5. NATURE : Soft, liquid, oily, heavy, crystal white, milky-white, sweet smell, no bad smell, sticky, plenty, colour like ghruta (Ghee), tail (Oil), honey.

6. SAAR : Soft, Watery eyes, Danta - Sama (equal Teeth) etc. Voice pleasant, colour pleasant , Big Buttocks, Strong, Healthy.

7. QUANTITY : Half Anjali

8. FUNCTION : Fertilisation, Dhairya, (Courage) Youth, Love , Happiness, Body Strength

9. UPADHATU : ----

10. MALA : ----

(5). UPADHATU

1). TWAK : (Skin)

1. NAME : Twacha, Charma,

2. SITE : Exterior of body.

3. CONVERSION (PARINATI) UTPATTI : Shukra- Shonita Pachana, from good part of Mamsa, Twacha is formed.

4. TIME : As Mamsa

5. NATURE : Ghana, Acchadaka, Patlakar, Tanu, Mrudu. Type - i) Udakadhara, ii) Asrukdhara, iii) Sidhma Kilassam, Bhavadh, Sthana. iv) Kushtha,

Mahavana, Phishthana, v) Alaji-Vidradhi, Sambhavadhshithana, vi) Chhinayam, Tamyati.

6. SAAR : As Rasa sara.

7. QUANTITY : Not mentioned

8. FUNCTION : Lepana, Kanti (Lustre) , Ushna sparsha (hot to touch), Bhrajaka Pitta, digests Lepa, Abhyanga.

9. UPADHATU : No as it is Updhatu.

10. MALA : No mala in twacha.

1A) TWAK LAYERS

	NAME	SIZE	ADHISHTHANA
1.	AWABHASINI	1/18 of VRIHI (Yava)	Sidhma
2.	LOHITA	1/16 of Vrihi (Yava)	Tila, Kalka, Vyanga
3.	SWETA	1/12 of Vrihi (Yava)	Charmadala, Ajagallika, Mashka
4.	TAMRA	1/8 of Vrihi (Yava)	Kilas, Kushtha
5.	VEDINI	1/5 of Vrihi (Yava)	Kushtha, Visarpa
6.	ROHINI	1 of Vrihi (Yava)	Granthi, Apachi Arbuda, Galaganda
7.	MAMSADHARA	2 of Vrihi (Yava)	Bhagandhara, Vidradhi, Arsha.
		= 5 Yava + 19/20	

2) ARTAVAM : Menstrual Fluid.

1. NAME : Artavam, StreeShonita, Rajahpushpa, Beeja - Rakta.

2. SITE : Garbhashaya (Uterus), Artavavahi (Follopian tubes), Artavavahini - Dhamani, Yoni (Vagina), Antargata Phala (Ovary).

3. CONVERSION : From Rasa Dhatu

(PARINATI) UTPATTI

4. TIME : 12 Years to 45 years of age. Rutukala, Rajahsrava kala (Menstrual Period).

5. NATURE : Rasasya Upadhatu, Agni - Soma yukta.

6. SAAR : Shuddha Artava, Garbha Janana, Samartha (Capable of fertilisation).

7. QUNATITY : Four anjali.

8. FUNCTION : Garbha Janana (Fetus formation), Stana Peenatwam (enlargement of Breast)

9. UPDHATU :

10. MALA :

3) STANYAM : Breast Milk

1. NAME : Stanya, Present in Stana, (breast) Dugdha (Milk) for child.

2. SITE : Stana - Two Stanavahi Dhamani (Lactaels). Stanavaha Srotasa (Payopavaha Srotasa) (Dugdha

Harini Nadi)

3. CONVERSION : From Rasa
(PARINITI) (like Shukra every where in body)
(UTPATTI)

4. TIME : One day , from Ahara rasa

5. NATURE : Like milk of cow, Shweta (white), Snigdha (oily), Guru (heavy), Madhura (sweet), can be mixed very well with water.

6. SAAR : ----

7. QUANTITY : Two Anjali.

8. FUNCTION : Strength to breast, Life for child

9. UPADHATU :

10. MALA :

OJA

1. NAME : OJA, Tejaswi dhatu,

2. SITE : All body, Hrudaya pradhana, Ten Ojovaha Nadi.

3. CONVERSION : Best part of all dhatus
(PARINITI) UTPATTI

4. TIME : ----

5. NATURE : Slight blood coloured and slight yellow coloured ghee coloured , Sweet, Guru (Heavy), Sheeta (Cold), Mrudu (Soft), Shalakshna, Bahula, Sthira, Prasanna, Snigdha (Oily),

Picchila (Sticky).

6. SAAR : ----

7. QUANTITY : 8 drops (Shleshmika) 1/2 Anjali.

8. FUNCTION : Jeevana, Ojonasha - Prananasha, Body stability. Oja - strength.

9. UPADHATU : ----

10. MALA : ----

8. MALAS (WASTE PRODUCTS)

1) PURISHA (faeces)

1. NAME : PURISHA

2. SITE : Malashaya - Rectum - Pakwashaya.

3. UTPATTI : By Purishdharakala in Sthoolantra - Unduka. (Large Intestine)

4. TIME : After digestion

5. NATURE : kittam (Solid faecal matter)

6. QUANTITY : ----

7. FUNCTION : Carry Annakitta(food waste)

2) MUTRA (Urine)

1. NAME : Mutra (Urine)

2. SITE : Vrukka (Kidney) Urinary bladder (Basti) Mutravaha Strotasa (Urinary Tract)

3. UTPATTI : by Mutravaha Srotasa (Urinary

		System)
4.	TIME	: After digestion.
5.	NATURE	: Liquid , Yellowish (Ambar coloured)
6.	QUANTITY	: ----
7.	FUNCTION	: Kledavaha (Carry waste)

3) SWEDA

1.	NAME	: Sweda (Sweat)
2.	SITE	: Swedavaha Srotasa (Sweat carrying channels)
3.	UTPATTI	: Due to Medagni, (enzymes of fatty tissue) Medapachanante Sweda. (Sweat at the end of digestion of Lipids)
4.	TIME	: ----
5.	NATURE	: Liquid, Oily, yellowish, soft, strong odour.
6.	QUANTITY	: ----
7.	FUNCTION	: Softness to Hairs , Skin.

■■■

DHATU AT A GLANCE

Sr. No.	Dhatu	Agni	Oja	Upadhatu	Dosha	Mala
1.	RASA	RASA AGNI	RASA	STANYA, RASA	KAPHA	Salviva, Tears, Sweat over cheeks
2.	RAKTA	RAKTA AGNI	RAKTA	SIRA, KANDARA (fascia)	RANJAKA PITTA	
3.	MAMSA	MAMSA AGNI	MAMSA	VASA (Muscle fat) Skin	KAPHA	- Wax in ear - crust in nose - denuded epithelium of skin - mouth secretions - tartar of teetch - denuded epithelium of intestine and conjunctiva

4.	MEDA	MEDA AGNI	MEDA	SNAYU, SANDHI, SWEDA (Sira - Sharangdharas (Sh))	KAPHA	- Sweat, Smegma of prepuce
5.	ASTHI	ASTHI AGNI	ASTHI	Teeth (sh)	VATA	- Nails,
				Hairs		Ruchaka - (C.S.V.=
						Charak Sushruta
						Vagbhata)
6.	MAJJA	MAJJA AGNI	MAJJA	HAIR (Sh)	KAPHA	- oily coponent of -
				Waste products of bone		i) Skin - Sebaceus Secretions
						ii) Conjuctival secretions
						iii) mouth secretion
						iv) faeces
7.	SHUKRA	SHUKRA AGNI	SHUKRA		KAPHA	Oja (Vagbhata)

9. AGNI (FIRE) AND AAMA

Concept of Agni

(1) Agni is technical concept of Ayurveda. Agni, according to Ayurveda has specific meaning. It is actually a sort of energy and has its origin in one of the five pentads i.e. Panchamahabhootas, namely 'Teja' or Fire. Basic biological element Pittadosha is the medium for Agni to reside and flow with.

(2) An entity which converts or transforms any substance (esp. food) into substance of more advanced or of higher order, also which changes biochemically a crude or gross substance into a finer or more minute form is called Agni. Agni is very much essential for convertion of food or digestion of food.

(3) Agni is very important entity in the body. Life is dependant for its existence on food, water and air. But for their utilisation in the living being they are to be processed biochemically by agni. Agni is supposed by Ayurveda, to be a root cause of human health. When agni becomes abnormal i.e. becomes weaker or more intensified it becomes root cause of diseases says Ayurveda. In Ayurvedic therapeutics to bring abnormal agni to normalcy proves to be an effective way of cure. Luster of skin, strength, health, vigour, growth, digestion, vitality are dependant on normal state of agni. So it is called life itself.

(4) The raja derived from causal teja, present in the molecules of Hormones, stimulates specific enzymes. The raja particles, in the protein molecules of enzyme, in turn, stimulate pitta molecules, which are chemically active biological units responsible for chemical reactions. Even though, hormones and enzymes belong to the category of

pitta molecules, do not form structural and functional units of the body. They represent highly specialised pitta molecules, which contain large number of raja particles derived from 'causal teja' or energy element.

(5) Every single cell of the body is site of 'Kayagni' i.e. agni in the body & metabolic activity i.e. 'Chayapachayakriya' is going or in each and every cell of the body. According to innumerable varieties of cells the varieties of agni also become countless. But for the sake of convenience only thirteen varieties of Agni are considered. One Jatharagni, Five Mahabhootagnis or Bhootagnis and Seven Dhatu-Agnis come to total of thirteen.

(6) Jathargni - It is situated in lower part of stomach, duodenum, small intestine and pancreas. Its particles are present in 'Dhatu-agnis' and '5 Bhootagnis'. It is not perceptible but can be anticipated logically by its effects. It is powerful yet it is subtle and minute. It is supposed to be God of the body yet dependant for its existence and action on the normal functioning of Pran, Apan and Saman Vayus. Its function is digestion of food. So various secretions of stomach, small intestine, including duodenum, pancreas and liver called 'pachak pitta' can be called as vehicles of Jatharagni, which is actually an energy. Various food constituents, having six rasas, are converted into sweet, sour and pungent tastes. Also it breaks down food first in molecules of tridoshas and then atoms of five pentads i.e. Panchamahabhootas.

This Jatharagni is divided into -

(a) Natural type i.e. Swabhavika, which is the original sort, dependant on the prakruti i.e. constitution of a person and is stable portion of it.

(b) Changeable type i.e. Oupadhik type- It is unstable portion of Jatharagni and becomes more or less according to the effects of age, place, time (day, night & season) climate or atmosphere, exercise, drugs etc.

Jatharagni is also classified according to the effects of tridoshas as below :-

(a) Vishamagni - i.e. ever changing or unstable type. It is under powerful influence of Vayu and found in persons of Vatprakruti, who all from time to time suffer from indigestion.

(b) Teekshnagni - i.e. severe agni. It is under powerful influence of Pitta and found in people of Pittaprakruti. Generally such persons have powerful digestive power. But when teekshagni becomes uncontrollable it creates a diseased condition.

(c) Mandagni - i.e. weak agni. It is under the powerful influence of Kapha and found in the people of kaphaprakruti. These persons have delayed digestion and always suffer from indigestion

(d) Samanagni - i.e. balanced agni. It is normal and ideal condition of agni and is due to balanced influence of tridoshas and so rarely found.

(7) Bhootagnis - i.e. Agnis related to Five Pentads. They are five in number. They react on the food partially digested by Jatharagni biochemically and break down the molecules of the processed food into atoms, so that the dhatu-agnis can react on them and can convert them into seven dhatus. Another important function of Bhootagnis is to supply specific nutrients to five dnyanendriyas i.e. five organs of perception. Liver is supposed to be the main site of bhootagnis. They function as below -

Parthivagni i.e. Agni related to earth element separates atöms of earth from partially broken down food particles and supply the subtle atmos from them as nutrients to sense organ of small in nose. Likewise 'Aapagni' i.e. Agni related to water element nourishes sense organ of taste in the tongue, Tejasagni or agni related to energy element nourishes sense organ of sight in the eyes, 'Vayu-agni' or agni related to Air element nourishes, the sense organ of touch in the skin and 'Akashagni' i.e. agni related to space element nourishes the sense organ of hearing in the ears.

(8) Dhatu-Agnis i.e. tissue agnis. They are sevn in number and are active all over the body. Each dhatu has got separate and specific sort of agni and has got peculiar function e.g. i) Rasagni converts Aaharrasa into Rasadhatu, ii) Raktagni converts the atomic portion of Rasadhatu into Raktadhatu. iii) Mansagni converts the atomic portion of Raktadhatu into Mansadhatu. iv) Medagni converts atomic portion of Mansa into Medadhatu. v) Asthi-Agni converts atomic portion of Medadhatu into Asthidhatu. vi) Majjagni converts atomic portion of Asthidhatu into Majjadhatu, vii) and Shukragni converts atomic portion of Majjadhatu into Shukradhatu. Dhatvagnis control the microdigestion or Sookshmapachan.

Aama

Aama has been defined as ...

i. undigested or semi-digested food

ii. Mala-Sanchaya (the accumalation of excretions) and

iii. First vitiation of Dosha.

Generally, it is produced by diminished power of digestive juices (Mandagni), but it may also form at other levels of the Agni i.e. Bhutagni and Dhatvagni.

Aama may be produced at any level of digestion and metabolism. It is basic cause of the diseases. Great stress has been laid in Ayurveda on correction of the digestion. The word Kaya-Chikitsa means treatment of vitiated Agni as Kaya means Jatharagni and chikitsa means treatment.

■■■

10. VYADHI (DISEASE) & CHIKITSA (TREATMENT)

1. Vyadhi (Disease) and Its causes

The condition which causes uneasiness to Sharira (body) or Mana (mind) is defined as Vyadhi or disease. It is produced by the three factors viz.

i. Asatmyendriyartha Samyoga,

ii. Pradnyapardha, and

iii. Parinama.

i. Asatmyendriyartha Samyoga

a. The excessive (Atiyoga),

b. Faulty (Mithyayoga), or

c. No use (Ayoga) of the sense organs is called Asatmyendriyartha Samyoga. Constantly seeing of bright objects like sun, reading in the dark and not seeing at all are the examples of Atiyoga, Mithyayoga and Ayoga respectively.

ii. Parinama (Kala)

The seasons play important role in the health and its abnormality may disturb the equilibrium of Dosha. Excessive cold, heat or rain in their respective seasons is atiyoga; less cold during winter or less hot during summer is Ayoga; and hot during winter and cold during summer is Mithyayoga of Kala (Season).

iii. Pradnyaparadha

If the right thing is not done at the right time then it is called Pradnyaparadha. It is the root cause of Asatmyendriyartha samyoga.

The causes of the disease may further be divided into

two groups viz.

a. Bahya (extrinsic) and

b. Abhyantara (instrinsic).

(i) Errors of diet, (ii) Season, (iii) Unnatural use of sensory and motor organs are the Bahya causes. (i) Vitiation of Dosha, (ii) Dushya, (iii) Srotas, (iv) Agni are the Abhyantara causes.

2. Classification of Vyadhi (Disease)

All the diseases are classified into 3 major groups viz...

a. Nija Roga,

b. Agantu Roga, and

c. Manasa Roga.

The diseases caused by the vitiation of Vata, Pitta and Kapha are called Nija Roga. The diseases due to the trauma, bite etc. are Agantu Roga. Mental diseases are Manasa Roga.

The diseases are also classified in 3 groups viz.

i. Adhyatmika,

ii. Adhibhautika, and

iii. Adhidaivika.

i. Adhyatmika - Adhyatmika diseases are further subdivided into Adibalapravritta (hereditary), Janmabalapravritta (congenital) and Dosha-Bala-Pravritta (due to vitiation of Dosha).

Adi-Bala-Pravritta or hereditary diseases are of two types viz.

a. Maternal or Matruja, and

b. Paternal or Pitruja.

Janma-Bala-Pravritta (congenital) diseases are also of

two types viz.

a. Rasa-Krita which are due to the vitiaed Rasa, Rakta etc. of the mother, and

b. Dauhrudapacaraja which are due to the irregularlities in diet during pregnancy.

Dosha-Bala-Pravrutta diseases are produced due to the vitiation of the three Dosha-Vata, Pitta and Kapha.

ii. Adhi-Bhautika - These type of disease are also called Sanghata-Bala-Pravrutta diseases. They are produced by extrinsic factors e.g. injury, bites etc.

iii. Adhi-Daivika - These diseases are produced by natural forces beyond the control to the man. They are of three types viz. (a) Kala-Bala-Pravrutta, (b) Daivabala-Pravrutta and (c) Swabhava-Bala-Pravrutta.

(a) Kala-Bala Pravrutta diseases are produced by seasonal changes which may be due to the vitiated (Vyapanna) seasons or normal changes (Avyapanna) of the seasons.

(b) Daiva-BalaPravrutta diseases are produced by contamination (Samsarga) or accidental causes e.g. lightning, fall etc.

(c) Swabhava-Bala-Pravrutta diseases are produced by natural physiological processes e.g. old age, sleep, hunger, thirst etc.

3. Shat-Kriya Kala

During the disease process the abnormalities of Dosh pass through six stages viz. (i) Sanchaya (Stage of accumulation), (ii) Prakopa (stage of provocation), (iii) Prasara (stage of spread), (iv) Sthana Samshraya (Localisation), (v) Vyakti (disease manifestation), and (vi)

Bheda (chronicity or permanent pathological changes or incurability). These 6 stages are called Shat-Kriya-Kala or time for the treatment. It has been emphasised in Ayurveda to diagnose and treat the disease at an early stage, so that its complications may be prevented.

4. Chikitsa

Whatever is planned for prevention or elimination of the disease may be known as Chikitsa. It is of three types, viz. (a) Daiva-Vyapashraya, (b) Yukti-Vyapashraya, and (c) Sattvavajaya.

(a) DAIVA VYAPASHRAYA CHIKITSA consists of wearing the Aushadha and practice of Mantra, Mangala etc.

(b) YUKTI-VYAPASHRAYA CHIKITSA is being widely used for the prevention and elimination of diseases by the Ayurvedic physicians since time immemorial. This type of treatment consists of planning (Yojana) of dietetic regimen (Pathya) and medication.

(c) SATTVAVAJAYA CHIKITSA is specially useful for the mental diseases and it consists of Manonigraha i.e. control of mind.

The main object of Yukti-Vyapashraya Chikitsa is Yukti or Yojana which means planning. In this type of treatment of physician plans the ....

a) Aahara, b) Vihara, c) Aushadha, d) Matra, e) Kala etc. by taking into consideration - a. Desha, b. Kala, c. Causes, d. Symptoms, e. Signs, f. stage, g. complications, h. curability etc. of the diseases. Taking all these points in view, a physician whatever plans (by Yukti) for prevention or elimination of a disease is known as Yukti-Vyapashraya Chikitsa.

Taking the different Yukti into consideration, the physician plans two types of treatment depending upon the condition of the patient. These are ....

1. Shodhana, and
2. Shamana.

(A) SHODHANA CHIKITSA

The treatment planned for the elimination of increased and morbid Dosha from the body is known as Shodhana therapy. It is also termed as Pancha karma (five fold therapy). It consists of ....

1. Vamana
2. Virechana
3. Anuvasana Basti
4. Asthapana Basti, and
5. Shirovirechana (Nasya)

Before undertaking the above five purificatory processes some treatment is to be given, which is called Purva-karma meaning 'pre-treatment steps'. It consists of Snehan, (oleation), and Swedana (sweating). In the after-treatment steps the patient is taken to normal diet gradually and this is called Samsarjana Krama.

(B) SHAMANA CHIKITSA

The treatment in which the Kupita Dosha (vitiated Doshas) is pacified without eliminating it from the body is defined as Shamana Chikitsa. It is classified in two groups viz. (1) Apatarpana, and (2) Santarpana. Apatarpana Chikitsa consists of three measures viz. (a) Langhana, (b) Rukshna, and (c) Swedana; and Santarpana Chikitsa is divided in.... (a) Brumhana, (b) Snehana, and (c) Stambhana.

(i) (a) **Langhana -**

This type of treatment is prescribed in the disorders caused by the increased Kapha or Aama. It consists of .... (1) Pipasa, (2) Atapa Sevana, (3) Maruta Sevana, (4) Pachana, (5) Upavasa and (6) Vyayama.

(1) Vamana, (2) Virechana, (3) Asthapana Basti and (4) Shirovirechana are also included in it. Thus it is clear that from Ayurvedic point of view, only fasting is not Langhana. Any of the above mentioned measures may be prescribed for Langhana, taking into consideration the strength of the patient.

(b) **Rukshana -**

It is indicated in the disease caused by Aama, Urustambha etc. In this type of treatment Ruksha, Laghu, Tikshna drugs are used.

(C) **Swedana -**

The treatment which causes sweating is known as Swedana. It is indicated in the disorders of Vata and Kapha.

(ii) (a) **Brumhana -**

The treatment which increases the Dhatu is Brumhana Chikitsa. It is indicated in weakness and diseases causing debility.

(b) **Snehana -**

This type of treatment is particularly useful for disorders of Vata. It consists of administration of oily preparations.

(C) **Stambhana -**

This type of treatment is indicated in the diseases of Pitta, Agnidagdha, Atisara, Vamana etc. The drugs having Shita, Manda, Mruda, Slakshana, Ruksha, Sukshma, Drava,

Sthira and Laghu properties are used for this treatment.

The above mentioned treatment is done through Aushadha (medicine), Aahara (diet) and Vihara (treatment with other means excluding medicines and diet e.g. exercise, rest, etc.)

PATHYA

In fact, Ayurveda puts a great stress on the diet and diet habit which are called 'Pathya'. It has been mentioned in Ayurveda that if a person suffering from any disease follows strictly the regulation of diet (Pathya); he may not require medicine, but if he does not follow the regulation of diet (Pathya) : he may not require medicine, but if he does not follow the regulation of diet, medicine may be fruitless. Taking account of these, it is necessary to follow 'Pathya' in health as well as in disease.

Selection of items of food and diet in general is to be made according to .....

1. Rasa (Taste),
2. Guna (Properties),
3. Virya (Energy),
4. Vipaka (Ultimate Results),
5. Prabhava (Active principles of action),
6. Compatibility and incompatibility (Viruddha).

Other important factors of diet are method of intake of the food, the time of taking the food and Satmya (homologous) etc. Stress is also laid on purity of Vayu (atmosphere), avoiding pollution of water, Desha (habitat) and Kala (season) for prevention of epidemics (Janapadodhvamsa).

■■■

PART TWO

AAHARA : FOOD

Contents

11. DIETETICS AND AYUREVEDA

(A) Important Tips about Diet for Health

(B) Vishamashan i.e. Abnormal Diet

(C) Viruddhashan - Antagonistic diet (Incompatible)

(A) Ahar-Vidhi-Vidhan

Important Tips on Diet for Health-

(1) Everybody should select such diet which will be useful for the maintenance of health and prevention of disease.

(2) (a) Abnormal Doshas viz. Vat, Pitta and Kapha, (b) Vitaite Dooshyas viz. seven Dhatus and Three Malas. (c) Obstruction in Strotasas (i.e. channels), (d) Weakened Agni (i.e. Mandagni) and (e) Aam (i.e. indigested toxic food) are the five entities which are causative factors of disease. Abnormal, improper and unbalanced diet is responsible for these five factors.

(3) One should take only those food items which are beneficial to him and suit him or her. The quanity of the food should be moderate and also it should be taken at proper time to remian healthy otherwise ill health is inevitable.

(4) Before eating food he should clean his hands, feet and mouth., The dining table should be clean, so also the dishes, spoon, bowles, water containers and cooking utensils etc.

(5) The surrounding and atmosphere in the dining room should be clean, cheerful and fragrant. The clothes worn, while doing outdoor duties should be changed and clean

homely attire should be worn.

(6) Food should be freshly prepared and warm. It should contain food items representing six rasas or tastes (viz. Sweet, Sour, Salty, Pungent, Bitter and Astringent) in proper proportions. Warm food is tasty and it intensifies Jatharagni i.e. Pachaka Pitta and indirectly promotes digestion, push Vat dosha in downward direction and reduces excess of Kapha dosha

(7) Oily or fatty content in proper quantity is quite essential as it makes food tasty, promotes secretion of digestive juices i.e. Pachaka Pitta. It also prevents excess production of Vatadosha, nourishes the seven dhatus, increase strength, gives lusture to the skin, causes easy expulsion of stool and gases.

(8) Lunch should be taken after complete digestion of breakfast. Evening meals should be taken after complete digestion of lunch. Roughly interval between breakfast and lunch should be of 4 to 5 hours and that between lunch and evening meals should be of 5 to 6 hours. Evening meals should preferably be taken before sunset. And one should retire 2-3 hours after taking evening meals. Taking meals late at night and immediately going to bed produces indigestion, gaseous distention, hyperacidity and disturbed sleep.

(9) One should avoid Viruddhashan and Vishamashana. Viruddhashana produces skin diseases and Vishamashana produces digestive disorders.

(10) One should not eat food in a hurry or very slowly too. One should masticate and chew the food properly . One should enjoy food cheerfully and attentively. One should be aware about the quantity of food and stop eating,

when he completes his moderate quota, as per his/her requirement.

(11) One should see that half of the stomach should be filled with solid or semisolid food, one fourth should be filled with water and remaining quarter portion should be kept empty for air. This will prevent indigestion.

(12) While taking food items of different tastes, the sequence of taking them should be like this : Food items having sweet taste (i.e. madhura rasa) should be consumed first, then items having sour and salty tastes (amla and lavana rasas) should be eaten and then items of other tastes should be taken. Especially items having astringent taste should be taken at the end of meals.

(13) Dosage of food depends upon Age, Agni (digestive power), nature of profession or occupation from the viewpoint of physical energy consumed in it, constitution, season etc. So the dosage of food changes from individual to individual. Ideal or correct dosage of food prevents abdominal distention, pressure on cardiac portion of chest and ensures efficient functioning of all organs in general and sense organs in particular

(i) After taking food in correct dosage a person does not feel sleepy or slothy, instead he can easily engage himself in usual activity. He can actively move about, do manual labour, breath, normally and retains his normal stamina, zeal and vigour intact.

(ii) Taking food less than the required correct dosage reduces strength weight , stamina, vigour and vitality, because Vata dosha increases

(iii) If the dosage of food becomes heavier than normal

the person feels heaviness in the abdomen and chest, feels sleepy. His zeal and zest, vigour and vitality, interest in work are lost because Kaphadosha increases.

(14) Drinking water before meals leads to weakening of Agni which produces indigestion. If this habit continues for a long time it results in loss of weight. Drinking water immediately after meals produces increase in Kapha production, and if this habit continues for a long time it results in obesity. So by drinking a very small quantity of water while eating food and then drinking it in sufficient quantity 2 to 3 hours after meal is over, the Tridoshas are produced in normal amount and proper digestion and metabolism are the good results. Especially the persons with hyperacidity are benefitted by drinking water in this manner.

(B)Vishamashana i.e. Abnormal Diet

Vishamashana i.e. Abnormal Diet is of five types. Their details are as follows :

(1) Adhyashana (Repeated eating or frequent eating of food) :- To take a diet before the digestion of previous diet is complete. which takes, on and average 4 hours is called Adhyashana. So there must be an interval of at least 4 hours between two meals. The indications of digestion of previous diet are : feeling of lightness of body, the belching is without the smell of the food you have taken recently, excretion of stool and urine is normal, the mind is cheerful, genuine feeling of hunger etc. If food is taken, even if the above indications are absent or indications are exactly opposite, then there is every possibility of indigestion gaseous distention diarrhoea, constipation and hyperacidity etc.

(2) Asamashana - To take food at wrong time and that too in excess or in less quantity than normal dose. It means for the sake of convenience to take lunch before its scheduled time or to avoid or skip meals even though one feels hungry. Both the things produce digestive disorders.

(3) Samashana - It means to take such a meal which is prepared by mixture of beneficial and harmful substances together. Its examples are : : to take alcohol with milk products or to take honey with hot water . It aggravates the 3 doshas.

(4) Anashana - It means not to take food at all or to fast. If fasting is frequent there is increase in Vatadosha due to lessening or weakening of 7 dhatus. It casues lowering of strength, complexion , metabolic activity and also reduction of efficiency of mind, sense - organs and intellect. It produces destruction of Oja, weakening of life force and creation of Vataj diseases.

(5) Viruddhashana - It means to take food which, in many respects, is antagonistic to the well being of human being. There are so many factors taken into account, which are thought of in context with Vishamashan in general and Viruddhashan in particular. We shall think of them in the next topic.

(c) Viruddhashana - i.e Antagonistic diet.

It means the food ingredients which in properties, are antagonistic to the properties of 7 dhatus viz Rasa,Rakta, Mansa, Meda, Asthi, Majja and Shukra.

The following factors are taken into account in context with Viruddhashana.

(1) **Deshviruddha** - i.e. antagonistic in context with land.

The diet which has similar properties as those of the geographical region of the residence it becomes antagonistic e.g. in the dry or arid land (i.e. Jangal desh) dry, light and cold diet (i.e. Vataj food) is antagonistic and so is prohibited.

(2) **Kalaviruddha** - i.e. antagonistic in context with time or season e.g. diet having cold , dry and light properties is contra - indicated in winter as it is Kalaviruddha.

(3) **Agniviruddha** - i.e. antagonistic in context with Agni. e.g. Light food is contraindicated for a person having severe agni (i.e. Teekshnagni). Heavy food is contra-indicated for a person having mild agni (Mandagni).

(4) **Matraviruddha** - i.e. antagonistic in context with dosage. Some foodstuffs prepared by adding two substances in equal amount are contraindicated e.g. ghee and honey. Also diet taken in excess or in less amount than normal need are also contraindicated.

(5) **Satmyaviruddha** - i.e. antagonistic in context with suitability e.g. diet with hot, penetrating, oily(pittaja quality) and also non-vegetarian nature with alcohol (Tamasika type) is contraindicated for a person suited to sweet, soft and vegetarian (Satvik type) diet. This type of unsuited or unfavourable food will produce even Allergic Disorders.

(6) **Dosha Viruddha** - i.e. antagonistic in context with dosha. Diet predominated by the same dosha by which the constitution or disease is dominated is contraindicated, e.g. a person of Vataja constitution, or in whom there is increase of Vatadosha, a diet of dry, light and cold nature

(i.e. Vataja nature) is contraindicated.

(7) Sanskar Viruddha - i.e. antagonistic in context with food processing. Sanskar means processing food item to change its qualities e.g. roasting, frying, cooking on steam etc. Specific substances produce harmful qualities if undergo specific processing. Curds or Honey on heating become harmful to body.

(8) Veerya Viruddha - i.e. antagonistic in context with Veerya Viruddha - Veerya is a specific quality of a substance which produces hotness or coldness in the body while undergoing digestion e.g. a food item prepared by using milk and fish together becomes antagonistic as milk is of sheetveerya) (i.e. producing coldness) while fish is ushnaveerya (i.e. heat producing)

(9) Koshtha Viruddha - i.e. antagonistic in context with digestive power of gastro intestinal tract. e.g. a person having low digestive power of g. i. tract should not eat substances like cheese, sweet meats etc. which are heavy for digestion.

(10)Avastha- kram viruddha - i.e. Antagonistic in context with the stage or condition e.g. In old age a light , cold and dry diet is antagonistic as the age is dominated by Vatadosha.

(11)Pariharviruddha - i.e. antagonistic in context with sequences e.g. after taking medicated ghee or til oil as a snehan karma (i.e. lubricating procedure) hot water should be taken. If cold water is taken there will be strotorodha (i.e. obstructive disorders of channels) and various diseases will be created. Cold water should be taken after heavy food items prepared from wheat .

(12)Pakaviruddha - i.e. antagonistic in context with cooking . The food which is not cooked or partially cooked is contraindicated and so prohibited.

(13)Samyogviruddha - i.e. antagonistic in context with the process of mixing . e.g. mixture of fruits with sour taste and sugared milk is contraindicated. Aslo mixture of fish with curds, that of alcohol with sweet milk product are prohibited as they are antagonistic with each other.

(14)Hrudviruddha - i.e. antagonistic in context with liking. One should not take a food item for which the person has apathy . Also one should not eat his meals when he is not in a good mood and so does not want to eat.

(15)Sampadviruddha - i.e. antagonistic in context with quality of food. Overstale and overripened fruits, meat of diseased animal, artifically produced (by chemical manures) and of crossbred variety agricultural, poultry or cattle products are prohibited.

(17)Vidhivruddha - i.e. antagonistic in context with table manners. Food should not be taken when one is having mental worries. Because it creates indigestion. Eating food with uncleaned hands, making munching sounds while eating, talking or laughing loudly throwing food particles from the mouth all around etc. are bad tables manners and hence are prohibited.

(D)Eight specifics of Dietetics

Diet is planned considering the eight speific entities concerning diet and dietetics.

(1) Constituion - i.e. Prakruti - - Here the Prakruti of the food item (and not of the person having it) is to be dealt with. While thinking about constituion of the diet, its Rasa, Veerya, Vipak, Prakruti i.e. normality and Vikruti i.e. abnormality, Gurutva and Laghutva i.e. heaviness and lightness (concerning digestibility) are taken into account. The only for a particular person a beneficial and specific food items can be selected and also avoidable. harmful food items can be sorted out e.g. A person having 'Kapha prakruti' should eat substances having pungent, bitter and astringent tastes, heat producing (ushna veerya) i.e. having the resultant tastes same as above and not other wise that means he should avoid substances like curds, guava, banana etc.

(2) **Karana** - i.e. food processing by various ways. Pulvarisation, pounding, mixing, grinding, fermenting, heating, cooling or freezing, churning, frying , roasting etc. are the various food processings methods. They convert the original properties of the various food items. e.g. by churning curds and adding water to dilute it into butter milk, the Kapha increasing and oedema producing property of curds is converted into agni stimulating and oedma curing property of butter milk. Wheat and Rice are heavy for digestion but by heating they become of light quality i.e. easily digestible.

(3) **Samyoga** - i.e mixing of two or more food ingredients. The new food item produced by mixture is usually of different property than the properties of the ingredients taking part in the mixing process. Meat is heavy for digestion but becomes easily digestible if cooked with or eaten with papaya pieces. A substance prepared by the mixture of wheat flour, gram flour paste and jaggery called Puran is heavy to be digested but if eaten with ghee it becomes easily digestible.

(4) Rashi - i.e. dosage or quantity of diet.

Here a) Parigraha Rashi means dosage in context with all the food items served are taken into account as a total quantity. b) A Parigraha Rashi means dosage of particular food item which is one of the numerous items served in a meal

(5) Desh - i.e. a specific agricultural land which produces a particular substance. According to the climates chemical composition of the land and the availability and quality of water, the specific agricultural product of a specific land is better than which is produced on land of another region e.g. Wheat from Punjab, Apples from Simala, Rice from Kerala or Konkan is of high quality.

(6) Kala - i.e. Time Factor . Kala has two varieties.

(a) Nityag Kala - It means the concept of time measured in units of second, minutes, hours and also seasons.

(b) Aavasthika Kala - it means various stages of Age of a person and also duration of a disease. Food , selected in context with season, age, and stage of a disease are beneficial to the body e.g. in enteric fever light and liquid diet is beneficial; so also food of tonic and nutrirtious diet in chronic fever. In old age rejuvenating and nutritious yet light diet should be given.

(7) Upayogasanstha - It means to take selected food according to the rules and regulations and factors concerning diet and dietetics.

(8) Upayokta - It means person taking food. Everybody should select his food taking into account his age, agni, individual suitability (satmya), digestive power of G.I.Tract etc. In the diseased condition what is beneficial in context with that particular disease should be taken and what is harmful should be avoided.

■■■

12. AAHAR PACHAN : DIGESTION

(I) Minute Digestion i.e. Sookshma Pachan :-

(1) Minute or microdigestion means further disintegration or splitting of bigger molecules of 'Aharrasa', the end product of Gross Digestion i.e. Sthool Pachan of food, to smaller particles, so that they can be resynthesized into specific tissue cells or Dhatu peshees, for the replacement of worn out cells of basic tissues i.e. 'Saptadhatus' and Tridoshas known to be Shareerbhavas.

(2) Human being cannot create food for his own use like plants. So he has to take vegetarian or nonvegetarian food items so that he can get raw or basic material, from which he can create substances, which are very much useful for his existence and maintenance.

(3) The raw or basic material derived from food material is of quite different nature from biochemical viewpoint. Every food item is made up of bigger molecules which again are made up of minute atoms of Five Basic Elements i.e. Five Primordials or Pentads called Panchamahabhootas.

(4) Disintegration of food first into bigger molecules and then into minute atoms is catabolic activity, while resynthesis, from the atoms, of seven categories of tissues i.e. saptadhatus and three basic biological elements i.e. Tridoshas is anabolic activity. Metabolism includes the

catabolic and anabolic activities. In short Sookshma Pachan i.e. microdigestion is mostly similar to Metabolism.

(5) For these catabolic and anabolic activities various types of 'Agnis' are required. 'Agni' is active energy principle of Pittadosha and it controls various biochemical processes. Vayu element or Vatdosha helps in carrying the splitting or catabolic activity while kapha dosha helps in binding or resynthesis of atoms i.e. anabolic activity.

(6) Sites of these catabolic and anabolic activities are numerous and are spread all over the body. In Ayurveda, these sites of various metabolic activities are called Srotasas. Srotasas are classified according to their specific functions. Each type of srotasa is having a specific type of agni and specific type of function. Modern concept of enzyme is very much similar with the concept of agni.

(7) From 'Aahar-Rasa', (Nutrient fluid) which is end product of gross digestion of food, the Rasadhatu is formed with the help of Rasagni, the Rasavahastrotasa. Rasadhatu thus formed has three parts viz. 'Sthool-bhaga' i.e. Gross portion, 'Sookshma-bhaga' i.e. Atomic portion and Malabhaga i.e. 'Residual Portion'. From Gross portion Rasadhatu proper and Upadhatus viz. Stanya i.e. Breast Milk and Raja i.e. Menstrual Flow are produced. From Atomic Portion 'Raktadhatu' is formed and from Residual portion 'Kapha dosha' and 'Kleda' minute dhatumala are formed. Likewise dhatus of upper or higher order are formed and at the same time their Upadhatus and Malas are produced from the gross, atomic and residual portions of dhatus of prior lower order respectively.

(8) The conversion of food stuff into different tissues of the body is controlled by three peculiar theories. All the ingredients or components of food change after undergoing

biochemical actions on them, is suggested by 'Ksheerdadhi Nyaya' or Milk-Curd theory and is example of 'Sarvatma-Parinamana' i.e. biochemical change of all the food components. The transferrence of food ingredients from Gastro Intestinal tract to each and every tissue upto the skin is suggested by Kedarkulya Nyaya' i.e. theory of 'Irrigaion of water from well to different pieces of a land through canals'. This is an example of 'Kramparinamana' i.e. nourishment of different tissues sequentially according to their distance from G.I. tract. Selective absorption of homogenous components and rejection of heterogenous components is according to 'Khale-Kapot Nyaya' i.e. 'Pruthak Parinamana' or 'Anshansha Parinama'. This theory suggest picking and carrying of particular food grains by pigeons from a farm.

(9) Rasa, Rakta, Mansa, Meda, Asthi, Majja, Shukra and oja is the sequence of synthesis by which tissue of lower order, builds from atoms of its own finer portion i.e. 'Sarabhag' the next tissue of higher order e.g. Rasa creates Rakta etc. But when time demands the reverse action takes place Rakta dhatu breaks down to balance the deficiency of Rasa dhatu. It can be concluded that tissue of the higher order can nourish the tissues of the lower order and so Oja can nourish all the seven tissues as and when necessity demands. This reversibility and interchangiability is the peculiarity of microdigestion and it is due to the basic fact that every cell in the body is made up of atoms of five basic elements i.e. Panchamahabhootas. In modern medical science also interchangibility of Carbohydrates, Proteins and Fats is demonstrated. Chakradatta puts it as Parapar-dhatu-sneha i.e. Mutual Co-operation of tissues.

■■■

13. JALA (WATER)

Introduction :

75% of the earth is covered by water & the 60% of our body is made up of the water. From Mahabhautic view point quantitatively water is the second largest Mahaboot after the air it is also second most important substance essential for the survival of living being after the air on this planet. The most basic nutrient needs is for water, the most abundant chemical in the body. Water is so vital for all body process that thirst impels us to drink long before our Water Level, becomes dangerously low.

Water As An Essential Nutrient.

Water is a very special kind of nutrient, it must be consumed at most frequent intervals & in greater amounts than is true for any other nutrient. It is common for example to need 2500 ml which is equal to 2 1/2 quarts of water in a day, while an intake of more than 500 gm carbohydrate in a day, is quite unusual & intake of other nutrients is very much smaller. Nevertheless, water is often overlooked as a nutrient. This is probably because the body has such good mechanism for stimulating appropriate water consumption that under normal circumstances healthy people automatically adjust their water intake to meet their needs.

Body Functions :

Water serves as a solvent, a component of all cells & body fluids, a means of regulating body temperature & a lubricant. Fifty to seventy percent of adult body weight is water ; the amount varies inversely with the proportion of body fat. The water content of the body, expressed as percent of body weight, falls with age. This holds true for adults even if they do not gain adipose tissue.

Water is the solvent in which most of the chemical reactions of the body occur. Its fluid properties allow it to serve as a medium for transporting vital substances throughout the body via the blood, lymph & other body fluids, & for eliminating wastes from the body. Water helps to provide lubrication in strategic location of the body (e.g. the synovial fluid in the joints & the mucus in the respiratory passages) Because it contributes turgor to cells & to the eye, water can be considered to provide structure. Regulation of normal body temperature is possible because water's unique properties result in significant cooling when water evaporates from the skin.

Dietary Sources Of the Water :

There are more sources of water available to the body. Beverages of any kind have a high water content. Most food contains a high % of water, including some foods that appear quite dry, such as bread & meat. Melons, celery, & many other fruits & vegetables contain about as much or sometimes more water than milk.

Metabolic breakdown of food for energy is an even less obvious source of water. The end products of the oxidation of energy nutrients are carbon dioxide & water. The amount of water produced endogeneously. i.e within the body is small as compared to that consumed in the diet. But it gains significance when the intake of water needed be limited.

The amount of water produced by oxidation of energy nutrients depends on the nutrient involved as follows : 100 g fat produce 107 ml. water, 100 gm. Carbohydrate produce 56 ml. water, 100gm protein produce 41 ml water. If a person's daily energy expenditure is 2000 kcal, his endogenous water production would be approximately 230ml.

Recommended Intake :

The need for water varies widely with variations in characteristics of the person's physical activity & the environment. A normal person can readily excrete excess of water via the urine if intake exceeds the requirement. The minimum requirement for a resting healthy 70 kg adult at moderate environmental temperature & humidity is about 1700 ml to 1800 ml per day. Normal activity can be expected to increase this requirement. The food & nutritional board of USA suggests that 1 ml/kcal is a reasonable water allowance for adults under ordinary circumstances. This value would be too low for those who are curbing their caloric intake. A higher ratio those who are curbing their caloric intake. A higher ratio namely 1.5 ml/kcal is recommended for healthy infants.

To be within a desirable range, intake of water should exceed the minimum required for replacing obligatory losses. An ample water intake helps maintain normal water content of the faces and thus promotes regular bowel movements. If water is in short supply, extra is absorbed from the colon. A generous water intake may also help to prevent uninary tract infection & kidney stones by increasing the flow of urine.

Individuals normally experience little day to day variation in water content. The body can't tolerate much fluctuation, because change adversely affects the concentration of dissolved substances & the integrity & functioning of cells.

Nutrients & Water

Protein :

Normal distribution of water between the blood plasma & the interstitial fluid requires a normal level of serum protein, particularly the protein called albumin. In turn a normal serum albumin level depends upon adequate intake of protein & calories. Serrum proteins influence fluid balance by their osmotic effect. They tend to draw water back in to the blood from the intestinal fluid. This may seem suprising since proteins are large molecules. Actually the large size of the molecules is responsible for proteins powerful effect on fluid balance.

If very low protein diet were consumed for a period of time the serum albumin level might fall so much that fluid would collect between the cells, increasing the total body water. However, changes in dietary intake of protein may not cause observable changes in water balance for weeks or months, while changes in sodium & on carbohydrate intake cause shifts in water content of the body within a matter of hours.

Carbohydrate :

Cadrbodydrate content of the diet affects sodium & fluid balance. A net loss of sodium & fluid occurs when carbohydrate is absent from the diet or in low supply as during starvation or adherence to low carbohydrate reducing diet. Putting carbohydrate back in to a diet leads to a regain of fluid & sodium, similar responses have been reported when carbohydrate content of the diet is changed without changing caloric intake.

Sodium :

The human body tolerates a wide range of deietary intakes of sodium. However, when there is extra sodium present in the body, the sodium tends to hold water with it. Thus extra sodium (salt) may increase the water content of the body. Although fluid retention may not be noticeable. Cutting down on salt intake cause many people to lose a little weight (fluid).

Water in Diseases :

Dehydration is nothing but the water deficit or volume depletion in human body. Illness & injury greatly increase the possibility that a person will develop dehydration Individuals who loose extra fluid because of illness seldom increase their fluid intake on their own. Those who are not encouraged to take liquid may quickly develop dehydration. This is especially true of the very young & old.

Diarrhoea :

Continued vomiting &/or diarrhoea such as often accompanies gastrointestinal upset is very common cause of life threatening dehydration in infants, young children & elderly. Dehydration caused by diarrhoea is one of the leading cause of death in children under four years of age throughout the world.

Uncontrolled Diabetes Mellitus :

When a person loses large amount of glucose in the urine, urine volume increases dramatically. Consequently, large amount of fluid are lost, Although thirst usually increase, it may not increase enough to cover losses. Persons who have diabetes mellitus not only need to have their glucose level regulated, but they need assistance to adequately replace fluid losses by use of sugar free fluids.

Diabetes Insipidus :

Individuals with diabetes insipidus are unable to concentrate their urine owing to lack of or resistant to antidiuretic hormone. These persons must drink large volumes of water daily unless their condition is satisfactorily controlled by treatment. Their fluid requirement (& polyurea) can be decreased by decreasing dietary intake of sodium & of protein.

Renal Calculi :

Increasing urine volume is very beneficial in the treatment & prevention of recurrence of renal calculi. Diluting the urine decrease the concentration of ions. The lower the concentration of the involved cations or both, the lower the likelihood that the salt will precipitate out in the urine to form a stone . Increased urine flow increases the possibility that crystals will be washed out of the urinary tract rather than having an opportunity to increase in size.

Urinary Tract Infection :

Increasing fluid intake & frequent voiding promote urine flow. These measures help prevent growth of bacteria & other micro organisms in the urinary tract. High fluids intake also serves to dilute irritating substances produced by micro organisms & thus to decrease tissue damage.

Chronic Obstructive Respiratory Disease :

For persons who have cough, adequate systemic hydration is important in liquifying secretions so they may be removed with minimum coughing. Unless contraindicated by other medical problems such as CCF pataints should be encouraged to drink enough fluids to produce thin, clear secretions.

Primary Water Depletion :

Primary water depletion occurs less commonly in clinical practice than sodium depletion & usually arises because water intake is reduced below an amount necessary to maintain the balance. This is liable to occur in patients who suffer from dysphagia or have obstructive lesions of the cesophagus or more simply in those who are comatose, depressed or apathetic, as is common e.g. in aged. Water deficit then occurs because the intake falls below the amount being lost from the lungs & the skin. This obligatory daily loss of water from the lungs & skin is increased by hyperpnoea or pyrexia. Excessive loss of water in the urine is a less common cause of water depletion such as in hyperparathyroidism & diuretic phase of nephrotic syndrome, nephritis etc.

Physical Activity And Water :

During vigorous physical activity athletes need to pay attention to their water needs. The body rids irtself of the heat produced during exercise via perspiration. Large water loss accompanying physical activity may lead to dehydration. The risk of dehydration is great in athletes who train hard or compete on a hot day. Increasing water consumption helps to prevent or alleviate this problem. Satisfaction of thirst is not always reliable indicator that water needs have been met. Frequent, scheduled drinking of plain water, juices, or other non diuretic beverages may be necessary to assure adequate fluid intake significant water loss may occur also in wrestlers who use dehydrating techniques e.g. sweating, vomiting, diuretics, & some rapid weight loss diet to stay within a certain weight range.

Water Intoxication :

Healthy individuals can safely drink very large volumes of water & respond to this by a vigorous water diuresis. The capacity of the body to excrete water when given without electrolytes is dependent upon many factors which include rate of glomerular filtration & the power of the distal tubules of the kidney to produce dilute urine. Many patients who are ill for a variety of reasons have a restricted ability to dilute the urine when given large amounts of water . These include patients suffering from acute & cronic renal disease, severe heart failure, adrenocortical insufficiency & hepatic cirrhosis . Occasionally tumors of the lung or ovaries secrete a polypeptide with antidiuretic properties which lead to water intoxication post operative subjects are also incapable of diluting the urine because of the liberation of vasopressin by the stress of the operation. In all these circumstances even a modest water intake reduces the plasma osmolality & the concentration of sodium & produces symptoms which are primarily those of disordered cerebral function; these include dizziness, headache, nausea & mental confusion. Severe water intoxication can produce convulsions, coma & death.

Water In Ayurved :

Differemt synonims for water are used by the brilliant scholars of Ayurved representing either the properties of the water or importance of the water in human life. Jeevanam is a synonim for water which means life. Life could not exist on this planet without water. For an Ayurved physician water is not only an essential nutrient but is one among the five basic elements essential for the creation of this universe. It is Jalamahabhoot.

According to charaka drava i.e. liquid, snigdha i.e. unctuous, sheeta i.e. cold, Mrudu i.e. soft, picchil i.e. sticky & Rasa i.e. taste are the attributes of the substances predominately made up of Jala Mahabhoot. Upakled (moistening) sneha (unctuous), bandha (binding), vishyanda (oozing), mardav (softening) & pralhad (exhilaration) are the effects of Jaleeya edible substances on the human bdoy.

Rasa i.e. taste is also an attribute of Jalamhabhoot. According to caraka water is the basis of taste. The water is basically tasteless but as soon as it falls from the sky gets endowed with the properties of five bhutas, or comes in contact with the other substances the taste or rasa appeared in the water.

Classification Of Water :

Charaka while describing the various types of water mentioned that, entire water is only one which falls down as rain from the sky. that while falling or having fallen down depend on place & time. He further says that water while falling down from the sky & coming in contact with the moon the air & the sun which follows time, gets impregnated with the properties of cold, hot, unctuous, non unctuous etc. & so when it rests on the ground.

Soil & The Water :

According to Charakacharya the pure rain water has by nature these six qualities sheeta i.e. cold, shuchi i.e. pure shivam i.e. wholesome, Mrishtam i.e. palatable, vimalam i.e. clean & laghu i.e. light. But when water fall on the earth its properties changes according to the soil on which it has fallen. In white soil it become astringent, in pale it become bitter, in brown alkaline, in usara saline, in hilly area pungent, & in black soil it become sweet. The water from rain, hailstone and snow is tasteless.

The Season & The Water :

According to Charaka- (1) The fresh rain water of the rainy season is heavy i.e. Guru, abhishyandi & madhur & that of autumn is Tanu i.e. thin, laghu i.e. light, Anabhishywadi i.e. which does not block the channels in the body. (2) In early winter i.e. Hemant rutu water is snigdha i.e. unctuous, vrushya i.e.aphrodisiac, Balya i.e. strength promoting & guru i.e. heavy. (3) In Shishira i.e. later winter it is Laghu i.e. light & alleviates kapha & vata. (4) The water of Vasant i.e. spring season is kashay i.e. astringent, madhur i.e. sweet & ruksha i.e. rough. (5) In Grishma i.e. summer it is non blocking for channels i.e. Anabhishandi . The water dropped by the clouds in perverted seasons undoubtedly causes harm.

The River & The Water :

Charakacharya has described the properties of water from different reivers. Its a a huge ecological observation. It shows the height of oriental wisdom & the extent of echofriendly nature of oriental thinking.

The river originating from Himalayas & constantly used by the sages & having water obstructed, agitated & beaten are whole some & virtuous, says Charaka. (According to modern science the water agitated & beaten by the big stones in the bed of the river contains more oxygen). Those originating from Malaya, carrying stones & sand have clean water which is like necter. The rivers flowing towards west have clean water & are wholesome while those joining the eastern sea are mostly mild flowing. Water of the river flowing from pariyatra, vindhya & sahya cause diseases of head, heart & leprosy as well as fileria.

Other Sources of The Water :

Merits & demerits of water contained in oblong ponds, well, tank, springs, lake & streams may be decided on the basis of the piece i.e. whether they are situated in marshy, hill or arid region. The sea water which is suppose to be the house of god varuna saline taste, fishy smell & it a grravates doshas.

The Good Water & The Bad Water :

The water which falls from the sky is called as Aindrya Jala. It is the principal drinkable water. Best water is slightly astraingent, sweet, thin, non slimy, light, non rough & does not block the channels of the body says Charaka. The fresh rain water in the season of autumn should be used by the delicate persons using unctuous & too much in preparing various types of diet.

The slimy water having insects, putrefied, full of leaves, moss & mud, having abnormal colour & taste, viceous & foulsmelling is not wholesome. It should be avoided. It was known to Carakacharya that impure & contaminated water is also responsible for the spread or diseases especially in epdemics. That is why while describing the epidemic diseases he particularly mentioned that the water should be known as devoid of merits when it is excessively deranged in respect of smell, colour, taste & touch. Such water is too slimy, deserted by aquatic birds & animals, is very less in quantity & unpleasing.

Jala Mahaboot & Human Body :

While describing the predominance of Mahabhootas in human body in sharirasthan of Charak samhita Charakacharya clearly stated that ," the liquid, mobile, dull, unctuous, soft & slimy, rasa, rakta, vasa, kapha, pitta, mutra, sweda etc. alongwith rasa i.e. taste & gustatory sense are predominatly made up of Jala Mahabhut. These are the Jaleeya sharir bhava.

Udakavaha Srotas :

Srotas are defined as transporting passages of dhatus undergoing transformation, says Bhagavan Atreya. There are types of srotas as many as corporeal entities All corporeal entities don't arise on decay without srotas.

For udakavaha srotas, the orign is Talu & kloma. The symptoms of their affection are dryness of tongue, palate, lips, throat & kloma & excessive thirst one should know that the udakavaha srotas are affected. The sings mentioned above are the early signs sings of dehydration irrespective of the cause. It appears from the description mentioned above that the undakavaha srotas is meant for maintaining the water balance of the body.

Dehydration :

Thirst is an urge to drink the water. Water is so vital for all our body processes that thirst compels us to drink long before we get dehydrated i.e. dangerously low level of water in the body. Charakacharya, in his topic dealding with urge specifically mentioned that the urge of thirst should not be hold. Suppression of thirst gives rise to dryness of throat & mouth, deafness, fatigue, depression & cardiac pain. For which cold & gratifying drinks are recommended. It becomes easy to control the complications when thirst itself is alleviated . Hence one should overcome the thirst before it leads to so many other disorders.

Excessive thirst due to loss of fluid dries up the patient & Skills him instantly. Hence one should take rain water i.e. Aindra jala mixed with honey or other similar water. The ground water which is astringent in post diagestive fate i.e. vipaka, thin, light, cold, fragrant, of good taste & non blocking of channels should be considered as rain water.

Water In Disease :

In the 22nd chapter of chikistasthana Charakacharya has discribed the water intake in different disease conditions. According to charakacharya in conditions of thirst, burning sensation, fainting, giddiness, exhaustion, poisoning & raktapitta. naturally cold water is recommended. In sannipata, water cooled after boiling should be given. In hiccup, dyspnoea, actute fever, coryza, after intake of ghee, diseases of chest & throat, kaphaj & vatik, dissorders, unctuosness & just after evacuation, hot water is wholesome.

Intake of water is not wholesome in case of pandu, udar (Ascitis), coryza, prameha (Anaemig Diabetes), gulma (Tumor), poor digestion, diarrhoea & spleen enlargement. However, if the desire is intolarable one should take water in little quantity.

If afflicted with severe previous disease the patient is exhausted & desires water because of excessive thirst, he may die or be inflicted with some chronic dissorder. Hence he should drink water added with suger & honey or some other suitable & favourite preparation.

Water In Fever :

In condtion of thirst, hot water should be given in vatakaphaja fever. Thirst caused by wine & pitta, cold water boiled with bitters is advisable. Both the above types of water are appetiser, digestive, antipyretic, channel cleansing, strength promoting, producing relish & sweating & are wholesome.

Water boiled with musta, parapatak, usira, chandana, udichya & Sunthi & self cooled should be administered to alleviate thirst & fever.

Water In Kaphaj Gulma :

The patient of kaphaj gulma should use water boiled with laghu panchamool.

Water In Premeha :

A person suffering from prameha (Diabetes) should drink water processed with the drug of salasardai group or kusa or honey water or triphala water or expressed juice of triphala.

Water In Panduroga & Kamala :

For those suffering from panduroga (Anaemia) water boiled with sataparini etc. i.e. laghupanchamula & for those suffering from kamala (Jaundice) the grape juice & the juice of amalalki is recommended.

Water In Vomiting :

A water diphed with heated clod or earth is recommended in vomiting along with other medical preparations.

Water In Panchakarma :

In virechana karma, (Purgation) after taking purgative drug there is constipation & the impurity is discharged in little quantity & with delay, the patient should drink hot water. By this tympanitis, thirst, vomiting & constipation are pacified.

In siddhisthan it is stated that " hot water digest the indigested unctuons Substances, breakes kapha & carminates mind. Hence hot water should be given in emesis, purgation in niruha & anuvasana enema for pacification of vata & kapha.

Water Preparation :

Water prepared with different substances are mentioned in Charak samhita. To avoid the repetation these water preparations are discussed here inshort.

1) Shadangapaneeya

Water boiled with musta, parapatak, ushir, chandan, udichya & shunti is called as Shadangapañeeya. These six substances together as one part has to be boiled with 64 parts of water. The water should be filtered & allowed to cool. Shadangapaneeya is indicated in fever & kaphaj Gulma (Tumour).

2) Trinapanchamool Sadhit Jala.

This is indicated in trushna roga i.e. thirst. The water boiled with Trunapanchamool & mixed with suger candy or mantha is called as Trunapanchamool Sadhit Jala.

3) Mruttika sanskrut sheetal jala.

In thirst the water boiled with tender leaves of vata,

matulunga, vetas, roots of kush, kasha madhuyashti & dipped with red hot black earth is advised. This water is then filtered & allowed to cool for the use.

Water prepared with Laghu Panchamool, Bruhat Panchamool, Dashamool, Salasardi gana are also some other examples of the water preparation useful in different disease conditions.

Comparison :

There are some similarities & some gross differences in the modern & Ayurvedic approach towards the water. Both sciences are well versed with the importance of water in human life. They also know the effect of water imbalance on human body. They also know that contaminated or impure water causes diseases & pure water is essential for human life. According to modern science the rain water is sterile one. This fact is known to Ayurvedic physicians more than 2000 years. They called it as Aindrya jala.

The sign of dehydration are known to both the sciences & they advised early supplimentation of water. Only differences in Ayurvedic text we find that thirst is described as a separate disease. Today we don't know the exact reason behind it.

Use of water in diseases is known to both the sciences & they are mentioned in the previous pages.

Differences :

The explanation of role of water in body functions is different in both the sciences. Same is the case with recommended intake of water. According to modern sciences such things are generalised but in Ayurveda the approach towards such things is individualised.

In Ayurveda water is not only an essential nutrient but is one among the five basic elements of the universe. It is Jalamahabhoot. Ayurveda has classified the water under different headings & the properties of all waters are explained in Ayurvedic text. The properties of water according to soil & the season are mentioned in Ayurveda. Another important point is they have described the properties of different rivers from all over the India. These are all the peculiarities of Ayurvedic approach towards water.

The water intoxication & the relation between different nutrients & water are mentioned in modern dietetics. Such references are not available in Charak samhita. Physical activity & water, specially in athlets is studied in detail in modern science. There is no separate mention of water in sports persons in any Ayurevedic text.

Conclusion :

From the review of the literature mentioned above we can conclude that we can use water for human being, particularly for a ill person in better way if we study these two approaches & use it in clinical practice.

References :

A) Nutrition - Principles & Application in Health Promotion by Suitor & Crowley.

B) Charak Samhita.

1. Sutra 26/9
2. Sutra 26/39
3. Sutra 27/196-197

4. Sutra 27/198-199
5. Sutra 27/203-204
6. Sutra 27/209-212
7. Sutra 27/214
8. Sutra 27/201-202
9. Sutra 27/208
10. Sutra 27/215
11. Viman 3/6
12. Sharir 7/16
13. Viman 5/3
14. Viman 5/8
15. Sutra 7/21
16. Chikitsa 22/25-26
17. Chikitsa 22/57-58
18. Chikitsa 22/59
19. Chikitisa 22/60
20. Chikitsa 3/143-144
21. Chikitsa 3/145
22. Chikitsa 5/167
23. Chikitsa 6/46
24. Chikitsa 16/114

■■■

14. DUGDHA (MILK)

Introduction :

The oldest written records of the human race is Rigveda. But milk had already become an important article of food. The cow was also worshiped in Babylonia & Egypt about 2000 B.C. Hathor, the goddess who watched over the fertility of the land was depicted as cow. Over 50 references to cow and milk are found in the old testament & the promised land was described as a land flowing with milk & honey.

The soliders of Chenghis khan . Mongol emperor who conquered Asia & a large part of Europe in the thirteenth centrury, carried dried milk as a part of their ration. The first settlers in new world (America) made the mistake of not taking cattle with them. For example the mayflower didn't bring cattle & as a result of the lack of suitable food, especially milk, the death rate was very high. In fact, nearly onehalf of those who came in the mayflower, including every child under two years of age, died during the first winter on this continent. This mistake was recognised & afterwards the governor ordered that one cow & two goats should be bought over for each six people.

Cow Milk & Buffalo Milk - An Ayurvedic View Point :

Charak samhita is the oldest one in all Avurvedic tests. In the Sutrasthan chapter 27 of Charak Samhita the properties & the usage of cow & buffalo milk are described under the subclas ' Gorasa Varga' . The description is based on the Panchamahabhautic theory . The properties, subsequent mahabhoota & uses are as follows.

	Cow Milk		Buffalo Milk	
	Guna	**Mahabhuta**	**Guna**	**Mahabhuta**
1)	Swadu	Prithvi, Jala	Swadu	Pruthvi, Jala
2)	Sheeta	Vayu, Jala	Sheetatara	Vayu, Jal
3)	Mrudu	Jala , Akash	Mrudu	Jala, Akash
4)	Snigdha	Jala	Snigdhatara	Jala
5)	Bahal	Pruthvi	Bahal	Pruthvi
6)	Shlakshna	Akash	Shlakshna	Akash
7)	Pichchil	Jala	Pichchil	Jala
8)	Guru	Pruthvi	Gurutara	Pruthvi
9)	Manda	Pruthvi, Jala	Manda	Jala, Pruthvi
10)	Prasanna		Nidrakara	

Properties - Best among the tonics Rejuvenator.

Properties - Enhances Sleep & decreases excessive appetite.

In this description from Charak Samhita the Samhitakara has compared the Guna (Properties) of Cow's milk & buffalo's milk. So the buffalo's milk is Sheetatra (colder), Snigdhatara, (more unctuous) Gurutara (heavier) than the cow milk. The Sheeta guna belongs to Vayu & jala ,Mahabhuta, Snigdha guna belongs to Jala Mahbhuta & the Guru guna belongs to Pruthivi Mahabhuta. In short the buffalo ,milk contains more Pruthvi, Jala, & Vayu Mahbhuta than cow's milk.

It means though the Gunas (properties) are same in both the milk but their percentage & proportion with each other varies in the two types. This difference in the proportion of Mahabuta influences the properties of the milk. Pruthvi & Jala Mahabhuta are the causative factors of 'Kapha dosha' and hence buffalo's milk increase the ' kapha dosha' in the body. Because of this increase in kapha dosha it enhances the sleep & controls excessive appetite. On the other hand because of the proportionate composition of gunas & the balanced Panchamahabhutas the cow milk is described as the best among the tonics & as a rejuvenator.

Cow Milk & Buffalo's Milk - Modern View

As a food articles the proximate principles vitamins, aminoacide of the cow milk & buffalo milk is as follows (Values per 100 gm of edible portion)

	Cow Milk	Buffalo Milk
01 Moisture	87.5 gm	81.0 gm
02 Protein	03.2 gm	04.3 gm
03 Fat	04.1 gm	06.5 gm
04 Minerals	00.8 gm	00.8 gm
05 Fibre	-	-
06 Carbohydrates	04.04 gm	05.0 gm
07 Energy	67.0 Kcal	117 Kcal
08 Calcium	120 mg	210 mg
09 Phosphorus	90 mg	130 mg
10 Iron	0.2 mg	0.2 mg
11 Carotin	174 mg	160 mg
12 Thiamin	0.05 mg	0.04 mg

13 Riboflavin	0.19 mg	0.10 mg
14 Niacin	0.1 mg	0.1 mg
15 Total B6	-	-
16 Folic acid free	5.6 ug	3.3 ug
Total	8.5 ug	5.6 ug
17 Vit C	2 mg	1 mg
18 Choline	-	-
19 Total N/g/100 gms	0.51	0.69
20 Arginine	220	200
21 Histidine	170	130
22 Lysine	500	490
23 Tryptophan	090	090
24 Phenylalanine	320	270
25 Tyrosin	300	-
26 Methionine	160	170
27 Cystine	050	090
28 Threonine	280	300
29 Leucine	600	640
30 Isolucine	280	300
31 valine	400	380
32 Sodium	73	19
33 Potassium	140	90

1) If we consider the weight of both milks as a standard then the cow's milk is inferior in Protein. Fat, Carohydrates, Energy, Calcium, Phosphorus, Amino Acids, Cystine, Threonine and Leucine but it is superior in all most all vitamin contents and the remaining Amino Acids. But if we study this chart considering energy as a standard and compare both the milks of equal caloric value (e.g. 117 Kcal) then the amount of milk varies considerably. For 117 Kcal, we have to take 100 gms of buffalo milk and 170 gms of cow's milk. Then the cow's milk becomes superior to buffalo's milk in all respect.

2) Physicochemical differences:

Buffalo's milk normally has a higher PH (Acidity) Buffer value, density, viscosity & Fat globule size than cow's milk. All these makes buffalo's milk heavier for digestion than cow's milk.

	Characteristics	cow's milk	buffalo's milk
01	PH	6.6	6.7
02	Buffer value (at PH 5.1)	0.0359	0.0417
03	Density at 20⁰ c	1.0287	1.0310
04	Viscosity (cp)	1.86	2.04
05	Specific Refr. Index	0.2059	0.2061
06	Surface Tension	55.9	55.4
07	Acidity	0.14	0.15
08	Fat globule size (mm)	3.85	5.01
09	Phsphate (Units)	83	28
10	Ultraviolet Fluorescene	Paleblueish	Greenish yellow

3. Casein Differences :

It has been established that there exists distinct differences in the physico chemical makeup of casein from buffalo's milk as compared with that of cow's milk. The proportion of miscellar casein is greater in buffalo's milk, while that of soluble casein is very low. The particle size of the buffalo's miscellar casein is larger (135um) than that of cow's miscellar casein (90um).

4) Fatty Acid Composition : Buffalo's milk fat is higher than cow's milk fat in butyric, palmitic, strearic & oleic acids , but lower in caproic, caprylic, capric, lauric & myristic acids.

5) Mineral Salt Difference : Buffalo's milk contains more calcium & phosphorus than cow's milk. But at the same time calcium phosphorus ratio is higher (2.26) in buffalo's milk than cow's milk (1.96) . There are more cations (calcium & magnesium) in buffalo's milk, but fewer auions (phosphate & citrate). The soluble forms of calcium magnesium & citrate are lower in buffalo's milk than cow's milk. Among the electolities the sodium & potassium content of cow's milk is higher (73 & 140) than buffalo's milk (19 & 90)

6) Amino Acids : The tyrosin is absent in buffalo's milk is available in cow's milk in a sufficient amount. This absence of one amino acid makes the protein from buffalo's milk inferior to that of cow's milk. This amino acid tyrosin is very useful for proper functioning of brain along with other amino acids like Tryptophan etc. The bioavilability of cow's milk protein is better than the buffalo's milk protein.

The properties of cow's milk & buffalo's milk is described as 'Prasanna' i.e. delightful & 'Nidrakara' i.e. induces sleep respectively are the functions of brain. It is a need to study the effect of these milks in neurotrasmitters & brain functions in detail.

Discussion & conclusion :

From the discussion mentioned above, it is clear that the cow's milk is superior than the buffalo's milk. This is also clearly mentioned in old Ayurvedic texts like Charak Samhita. But the Ayurvedic claims doesn't end with the claim of superiority. Charackacharya clearly stated that cow's milk is one of the best among the tonics. Another property is it delights the mind.

Another important factor is pollution. Charak Samhita is 2000 years old. That time pollution was almost nil. No chemical fertilisers & pesticides were used. The cattles were fed on the green grass. There were no hormonal injections for increasing milk output. Todays cattles are fed on already polluted fodder & most of them are milking machines. All these factors affect the quality of milk. Charakacharya stated that, because the 'Guna ' of cow's milk & 'Oja' are the same, the cow's milk is the best among the tonics. i.e. Jeevaneeya dravyas.

REFERENCES

1. Charak Samhita — Vidyotinee Tika, Chaukhamba Prakashan
2. Outline of dairy Technology — Sukumar De, Oxford University press Delhi - 1994
3. Milk & Milk Products — C.H.Eckles, W.B.Combs & Herold Macy. Tata McGraw Hill Publishing Company Ltd. Delhi - 1994
4. Nutritive Value of Indian Foods — C Gopalan & others NIN - 1995
5. Diet, Neurotrasmitters & Brain Function — G.H.Anderson British Medical Bulletin - 1981 Vol. 37 No. -1

15. YAVAGU (GRUELS)

When we talk about dietetics we immediately remember the modern dietetics which is based on biochemistry. It is believed that it has some role in preventive medicine but it has nothing to do with curative part. There is a clearcut demarcation in diet & medicine. Some people have claimed that diet has a definite curative value but there is a dispute over it.

Old seers & sages worked over this for years together & reached some conclusions. We can find detailed description of different types of food & their properties in old Ayurvedic and religious texts. Not only that we can get references of general dietetics in books like 'Vatsyayan Kamasutra' and diet to be used in aviation in books like 'Nauka Nayan Shastra' and 'Yantra Sarvasva' etc. We also have separate texts like 'Bhojana Kutuhal' by 'Nala' on Cookery. But Ayurved has not described any person as a dieticians. An Ayurvedic physician has to play that role. It is totally his descretion whether to advice medicine or change in diet or both. Because of such combination some peculiar concepts and traditions were developed in Ayurveda. Medicated gruels described in charak samhita sutrasthan is one of them.

Charak Samhita is the oldest textbook on Ayurved. It is written by Maharshi Agnivesh and is reedited by Maharshi Charak. Another speciality of Charak Samhita is its importance in treatment. The speciality of charak samhita lies in its simplicity. Maharshi Charak has described very simple treatment for general ailments as well as the treatment of many complicated illnesses. Its position is still abated.

The classical example of its simplicity is the description of twentyeight medicated gruels (Yavagu) described in 'Sutrasthan'. Yavagu or gruel is a simple rice preparation. The rice has to be cooked with six times more water. The word 'Peya' appears to be the synonim of 'Yavagu' in charak samhita. These twenty eight yavagus are as follows :

1. Antispasmodic gruel (Shoolnashak Yavagu)
2. Digestive and astringent gruel (Pachani & Grahi Yavagu).
3. Anti diarrhoeal gruel (Vata) Atisaraghni Yavagu)
4. Anti diarrhoeal gruel (Pitta shleshmic Atisaraghni Yavagu)
5. Anti diarrhoeal gruel (Raktatisaraghni Peya)
6. Gruel useful in loose motion with mucus (Amatisaraghni Yavagu)
7. Diuretic gruel (Mootra krichraghni Peya)
8. Gruel for deworming (Krimighni Yavagu)
9. Anti thurst gruel (Pipasahar yavagu)
10. Anti poisonous gruel (Visha nashak yavagu)
11. Gruel useful in kachexia (Karshyahar yavagu)
12. Gruel useful in obesity (Medohar yavagu)
13. Gruel useful in oliation (Snehan yavagu)
14. Gruel useful in bringing dryness in the body (Rookshan yavagu)
15. Anticough, decongestant, gruel (Swaskasaghni yavagu)
16. Antispasmodic gruel (Pakwashaygata vataj shoolhar yavagu)
17. Laxative gruel (Rechani yavagu)
18. Astringent gruel (grahi yavagu)
19. Purgative gruel (Bhedani yavagu)
20. Gruel useful in promoting peristalsis (Vatanulomi Yavagu)

21. Gruel used as antidot for excessive oliation by Ghrita (Ghrita Vyapadhar yavagu)
22. Gruel used as antidot for excessive oliation by oil (Tail vyapadhar yavagu)
23. Antipyretic gruel in intermitant fever (Vishamajwaraghni yavagu)
24. Gruel useful in disease of throat (Kantharogaghni yavagu)
25. Antispasmodic gruel in urinary tract and seminal vesicals (Shukravahasrotas shool shamanartha yavagu)
26. Aphrodisiac gruel (Vrishya Prayogartha yavagu)
27. Gruel useful in alcoholism (Madarog harak yavagu)
28. Gruel useful in over eating (Bhasmak Roganashak yavagu)

The systemwise classification of these twentyeight gruels is as follows.

(1) Thirteen are related to digestive system. Out of thirteen. (a) Five have a specific indication against diseases like "Vataj Atisaraghni', Pittakafaj Atisargaghni' Raktatisaraghni, Amatisaraghni and in Bhasmak Roga. (b) 'Bhedani' and 'Rechak yavagu' have strong and mild laxetive action (Property) respectively. (c) Two are useful in pain in abdomen. One is 'shool nashak' and the other is 'Pakwashaya gata vataj shool Nashak'. (d) 'Krimighni' yavagu as its name indicates have anthelmentic property. (e) Grahi and Pachani has digestive as well as astringent property on G. I. tract & only 'Grahi Yavagu' is useful to stop the loosemotion.

(2) 'Mootrakruchaghni Peya' has diuretic property and 'Shukravaha Srotas Shool Shamanartha Yavagu; has antispasmodic & analgenic action on seminal vesicals as well as urethra.

(3) 'Shwasakasaghni' & 'Kantharogaghni Yavagu' is useful in asthama & general respiratory track complaints.

(4) 'Medohar' and 'Karshyahar' yavagu are useful in obesity and general debility respectively.

(5) 'Vishamajwaraghni' Yavagu as its name indicates is useful in intermitant fever. 'Vrishya Prayogartha' yavagu is supposed to be aphrodesiac in action.

(6) 'Snehan' 'Rookshanartha' 'Ghritavyapadhar' and 'tailavyapadhar' yavagu are for specific purposes and such type fo indications can come across only in Ayurvedic practice.

(7) 'Pipasahar yavagu' is useful in mild dehydration as well as in summer.

(8) 'Visha Nashak' yavagu may not prove useful in todays context but.

(9) 'Madarog Nashak Yavagu' is still worth giving trial even today.

Out of these twenty eight gruels, (a) Five preparations are nonvegiterian and (b) Twenty three are vegiterian preparations.

Nearly 44 herbal medicines are used in these 28 gruels. (a) Four types of grains. (b) Six substances of animal origin. (c) Four types of nonvegetarian soup & some other commonly available substances like oil, honey, salt & alcohol are used in these gruels.

Maharshi Charak has described twentyeight medicated gruels i.e. yavagu for different illnesses. Here the yavagu is used as a carrier of medicine. It is a very simple preparation. The ailments for which they are indicated are our day to day problems. Because of its form its acceptability by the patient is always better then any other preparation. The herbal medicines used here are easily available and there is no need of purification etc. There is no doubt about its safety. These are all time tested herbs. In other words these gruels are home remedies. Any person can prepare these gruels in his/her homes (home/kitchen pharmacy).

There is a story from a China. Once a king asked his chief physcian that 'who is superior to you'? The Physician-answered 'His Majesty, my elder brother'. The king said surprisingly that "I never heard his name". The royal physician said that he is known in our locality only'. The king asked, 'then what is his speciality?' The royal physician said, 'Sir he is very expert in detecting the disease in its very early stage and he cures it with very simple medicines.' Then the king said, 'he must be the best physician in our country !' The royal physician said 'no sir'. Again with surprise king asked 'then who is the best physician in our country'? The Physician answered 'His Majesty, my eldest brother'. The king said, 'I even don't know that you have one more brother. The royal physician replied, 'yes Sir, he is popular in our family members only. Because he has an ability to predict the probable illness of a person only by observing his food habit, and he can treat him only by little change in diet.'

Then finaly the king asked, 'then what about you'? The royal physician said, 'Sir I can diagnose the disease only when it is fully manifested and then I can treat it with number of medicinal preparations and massage, fomentation etc. That is why I became popular and now I am royal physician'.

Conclusion : Food as medicine is first choice.

■■■

16. DIET

A) Liquid Forms of Diet

1) Mand (Rice Water)

Intgradients	:	rice and pure water
Sanskar dravyani	:	dry ginger powder, rock salt
Procedure	:	Take one part of rice in a pan and add fourteen parts of water to it. Boil till the rice is completely cooked. Filter and take only liquid part. This is called **Mand.** Add two pinches of dry ginger powder and rock salt each, to the **Mand** and serve/take when hot.
Dosage	:	200 ml thrice a day for the 1st day. (According to the agnibala (digestive power) the dose can be altered in quantity and administration time)
Duration	:	Two days

Properties of Ingradients and sanskardravyani -

a) Rice -	-	It itself is easy to digest, tasty and **Agnivardhak**.
b) Dry ginger	-	This is tasty, digests indigested or semidigested food and works as powder

		Agnideepak.
c) Rock Salt	-	It is subtle and hot in nature, so it helps to digest semidigested or indigested food and also promotes the secretions in the digestive system. Thus increases the potency of **Agni**.

Properties of MAND

Mand itself is very easy to digest. It acts as predigest. It is **Agnivardhak**. Besides it give nutrition to tissues.

Note - It is advised to use brown rice or raw rice. Do not use polished rice. Ayurved says that rice grains harvested at the age of sixty days are ideal. This rice is called **Sathesal** or **Shalishashtik**.

2) Peya (Rice water with some rice particles)

Ingradients	:	Rice and pure water
Sanskardravyani	:	Dry ginger powder and rock salt
Procedure	:	Take one part of rice in a pan and add fourteen parts of water to it. Boil till the rice is completely cooked. This is **Peya.** The difference between **Mand** and **Peya** is in **Mand** only liquid part is, to be ingested while in **Peya** rice is ingested, too.
Dosage	:	200 ml thrice a day

Duration : One day.

Properties of Igradients and Sanskardravyani -

a) Rice : Itself is easy to digest, tasty and Agnivardhak.

b) Dry ginger : Is tasty, digests indigested or semidigested food and works as Agnideepak. Powder

c) Rock salt is subtle and hot in nature, so it digest the semidigested or indigested food and also promotes the secretions in the digestive system. Thus increases the Potency of Agni.

Properties of Peya : It itself is very easy to digest. It fulfils thirst and hunger. Provides nutrition to the cells/tissues and helps to recover from weakness. It stimulates the large intestine so that constipation if any, is releived. It's called as Agnijanani i.e. it creates (increases the potency of the Agni).

Note : For Peya brown rice, raw rice of Shalishashtik are advised as best.

B) SEMI SOLID FORMS OF DIET

1) YAVAGOO -

Ingradients : Rice and pure water.

Sanskardravyani : Ghee (clarified butter) powders of dry ginger, black peeper, cumin seeds and common salt or rock salt.

Saiṇdhav

Procedure : In a fry pan take one

tablespoon of clarified butter and add one part of rice to it. Roast the rice till it becomes pinkish brown. Then add six parts of water to it and keep boiling. When the rice is completely cooked a thick paste is formed. This is **Yavagoo.**

Then add two pinches of each of the powders-dry ginger, cumin seeds and black pepper - salt as per requirement of the Yavagoo and eat while hot.

Dosage	:	200 ml thrice a day
Duration	:	One day.

Properties of Ingradients and Sanskardravyani -

a) Rice	:	Is very easy to digest, tasty and Agnivardhak..
b) Ghee	:	(clarified butter) is Agnivardhak. Sitmulates and increases the Agni to some extent. The most important property of ghee is it's Yogavahi.
c) Black Pepper	:	(Piper Nigrum) is tasty, hot in nature, it has a property known as Pramathi because of which it can reach each

			and every cell and activate metabolism or digestion at cellular level, too. Hence, it works as Agnideepak.
d)	Dry Giner	:	Is tasty, hot in nature, kindles the Agni, digests semidigested food particles and works as Agnivardhak.
e)	Rock Salt	:	Is subtle, hot and very tasty in nature. It may be stimulating the centres for taste in cerebal cortex, as a result of which normal taste is regained.
f)	Common Salt	:	It has the properties similar to rock salt except that it is Abhishyandi in nature.
g)	Cumin Seeds	:	Are bitter and hot to taste, also aromatic and easy to digest. Cumin being hot in nature digests the semidigested and undigested food as well as stimulates the Agni.

Properties of Yavagoo -

Yavagoo it self is light to digest. It provides nutrition to the cells and acts as Agnideepak.

It is advised to ingest **Yavagoo** after having **Mand** and **Peya. Agnideepan** to some extent is achieved and then to promote the potency of **Agni** more and to fulfill hunger and provide energy to the body, **Yavagoo** is used.

2) YUSH

Ingradients	:	Green gram (Moong dal), water.
Sanskardravyani	:	Ghee (clarified butter) dry ginger powder, cumin seeds powder, rock salt, black pepper.
Procedure	:	Take one tablespoon of clarified butter in a fry pan. Then add part of 'moong dal' to it and roast till the 'dal' becomes pinkish brown. Then add eighteen parts of water to it and keep boiling. Cook the mixture till the dal can be meshed completely. Prepare a syrup like mixture by mixing the dal thouroughly in the water. Yush should be liquid in form but much thicker than Peya. Add powders of black pepper, dry ginger, cumin seeds and rock salt two pinches each. Serve while hot.
Dosage	:	200 ml twice or thrice a day.
Duration	:	One day

Properties of Ingradients and Sanskar Dravyani -

a)	Moong Dal	:	(Green gram dal) - It is sweet to taste (Rasa) and Vipak (effect which forms after digestion in the intestine). Cold in Veerya (i.e. active principle or potency. It's properties are as follows : Dry, light to digest and Balya (provides energy). Because of these properties it normalises the excess Kaphdosha and Pittadosh as well as provides essential nutrients to the body.
b)	Clarified butter	:	Ghee is Agnivardhak and Yogavahi.
c)	Black Pepper	:	Is tasty, hot in nature and Agnideepak.
d)	Dry Ginger	:	Is tasty, hot, kindles the Agni and by digesting the semidigested or undigested food helps to increase the potency of Agni.
e)	Rock Salt	:	Is subtle, hot, very tasty, Stimulates the centres for taste and works as Agnideepak.
f)	Cumin Seeds	:	Are bitter and hot to taste, specially aromatic. Help to kindle the Agni by digesting

the semidigested food. Also works as Agnivardhaka.

Properties of Yush are as follows :

Yush is tasty and develops taste, It is easy and works as Agnideepak and Agnivardhak. It is energetic but reduce excess Kaphadosha. It is nourishing as well as fulfills hunger and thrist.

Note : Yush can be prepared by using some other cereal or vegetables or medicinal plants, e.g. Red gram (Lentil) dal Chinese Dolicus, Rice etc. vegtables like ,carrot, tomato spinach can be used. Mediccinal plants such as Punarnava (Boerhvia) Ativisha (Aconite), Rasona (Alliumsativum) (garlic) may be used to prepare Yush. Fruit like (Dadim) pomogranate is used. Chiken & mutton soups can be included in Yush.

C) Solid Forms of Diet -

1) Vilepee -

Ingradients	:	Rice or any other cereal, water.
Sanskardravyani	:	Clarified butter, rock salt, cumin seed powder, black pepper powder.
Procedure	:	Take one part of rice.cereal in a fry pan, add four parts of water to it. Boil till the rice is completely cooked. Stir well. A thick and sticky paste will form, which is called Vilepee. Add one tablespoon of

		clarified butter and two pinches of each of cumin powder, black pepper powder and rock salt to Vilepee. Ingest when hot.
Dosage	:	200 gms. cooked Vilepee twice or thrice a day.
Duration	:	One day.

Properties of ingradients and sanskardrvyani -

a) Rice	:	Itself is tasty, easy to digest and Agnivardhaka.
b) Clarified butter	:	(Ghee) is Agnivardhak and Yagavahi.
c)	:	Black Pepper powder is tasty, hot in nature and works as Agnideepak.
d)	:	Cumin seeds are bitter and hot to taste, specially aromatic. Help to kindle the Agni as well as to increase the potency of Agni.

Properties of Vilepee -

Vileppee is Agnideepak, and it helps to restart the hunger phenomenan, i.e. it elimenates the nauseatic feeling, thus reduces anorexia. It is completely nourshing and specially useful in stregthening the heart as per Ayurvedic philosophy. It fulfills hunger and thirst, binds the faeces and helps in the excretion process.

Note : Vilepee can be prepared using any of the following substances - Wheat, Millete, Pearl Millete, Barley, Ragi etc.

2) Krishara - (Khichadi)

Ingradients	:	Rice and Moong dal (whole green gram can also be taken), water.
Sanskardravyani	:	Ghee (clarified butter), cumin seeds, Haridra (curcuma longa) (Turmeric), Hingu (Asafoetida) (Ferula narthex), capsicum, common salt.
Procedure	:	Take one tablespoon ghee in the fry pan and heat it. Add cumin seeds, Hingu, capsicum pieces and a pinch of Haridra one by one, to the hot ghee. Then add cleaned and soaked rice-moong mixture to it. Fry to ten to fifteen minutes till mixture becomes pinkish brown in colour. Then pour boiling water, double that of rice and moong mixture in the pan. Add salt and pressure cook for ten minutes. Stop cooking and serve hot.
Dosage	:	150 gm to 200 gm cooked

		Krishara, twice or thrice a day.
Duration	:	One day.

Properties of ingradients and sanskardravyani -

a) Rice	:	Itself is easy to digest, tasty and Agnivardhak.
b) Moong dal	:	Is sweet in Rasa, Vipak and cold in Veerya (i.e. potency to work). It is highly nutritious and energetic. Fulfils hunger, Acts as Agnivardhak.
c) Clarified butter	:	Agnivardhak and Yogavahi (see the key).
d) Cumin seeds	:	Bitter, hot to taste, specially aromatic. Help to kindle the Agni, as well as work as Agnivardhak.
e) Haridra	:	(Curcuma longa) Bitter and hot in nature and taste. It itself is tasty so eliminates nausea. Helps to digest the food.

f) Hingu (Asafoetida) (Ferula narthex) :

It is bitter to taste (Rasa) and Vipak also hot in Veerya (potency to work). Light/easy to digest, has penetrating capacity and is unctuous in nature. It helps in the process of digestion, besides works as Agnideepak and Vardhak.

g)	Capsicum	:	Teekshna and ushna due to which it works as Agnideepak. Helps to reduce nausea and anorexia.
h)	Common salt	:	It is subtle, hot, very tasty and may be stimulating taste centres. Slightly Abhishyandi (oozing).

Properties of Krishara -

KRISHARA is highly nutritious and energetic. It is heavy to digest as compared to all above mentioned forms of diet but lighter than chapati (bread) and other preparation containing pulses, vegetables, oils and spices etc. It produces normal essential good quality Kaphadosha and Pittadosha. It also helps normal excretion phenomena, reduces constipation and oligurea, if any. Krishara is Shukral i.e. increases normal semen quality to some extent. If it is ingested daily it reduces the aging process.

Note : Thus by using the above given receipies Agnimandya can be cured. This procedure is described as Samsarjankrama in the Ayurvedic texts. Dosages and duration of the Samsarjankrama can be altered according to the degree of Agnimandya, Prakruti and the pattern of increase in the potency of Agni. For example if pittaprakruti patient has Agnimandya, his/her sansarjana Krama will reduces from sven days to five days as his Agni is basically of Teekshna quality and will be recovered earlier than that of the other two Prakriti.

■■■

17. SANSARJANA KRAMA

Introduction :

The post Panchakarma dietary regime is called as sansarjan kram. In practice it is advised only Vamana & Virechaṇa Karma. No sansarjan kram is advised after Basti, Nasya or Raktamokshan. The reason is during vamana & virechana karma there is much stress on Annavaha srotas & the digestive fire gets slowed. Hence charakacharya has asked to follow the dietetic regime with Peya, Vilepi etc. in three, two or one meal time respectively according to the degree of evacuation like superior, medium or inferior.

As little fire kindled gradually with grass, cow dung etc. becomes great, stable & all digesting the internal fire of the evacuated one does like with peya etc.[1] says charaka.

Some peculiarities of sansarjan krama :

1) The duration of sanarjan krama depends on the degree of samshodhana.

2) The quantity of the preparation depends on the appetite of the patient.

3) Sansarjan kram should begin with liquid gruel (Mandayukta Yavagu) & endue with Odana with meat soup irrespective of duration of sansarjan krama.

4) A specific sequence of Rasa should be followed while preparing the gruels etc.

The Sequence of Sansarjan Krama after Vaman

Though the sansarjan krama depends on the degree of samshodhana, charakacharya described the full regime useful in superior degree of evacuation[2]

1) 1st Annakala - Mandayukta Yavagu i.e. lukewarm, scummy gruel of red rice.

2) 2nd Annakala - -------------------------- do ---------

3) 3rd Annakala - -------------------------- do ----------

4) 4th Annakala - Vilepi i.e. Paste like preparation of red rice with or without unucting substance & salt

5) 5th Annakala - -------------------------- do ----------

6) 6th Annakala - -------------------------- do ----------

7) 7th Annakala - Odana i.e. cooked rice + Yush i.e. dilute green gram soup + little uncting substance & salt.

8) 8th Annakala - -------------------------- do ----------

9) 9th Annakala - -------------------------- do ----------

10) 10th Annakala - Odana i.e. cooked rice + dilute bird's meat soup & salt.

11) 11th Annakala - -------------------------- do --------

12) 12th Annakala - -------------------------- do --------

After each meal warm water is adviced for drinking

In Short, mandayukta yavagu i.e. scummy gruel of red rice is advised for first three meal times. A paste like preparation of red rice with or without uncting substance & salt is advised for next three meal times. Cooked red rice with green gram soup & little uncting substance & salt is advised for next three meal times & cooked red rice with birds meal soup & salt is advised for last three meal times.

Here the quantity of rice is not mentioned but as a general rule we can follow the sushrutas advice. He advised 1/4th quantity of the daily requirement of a person while preparing manda, peya, vilepi or yavagu[3].e.g. if a person consumes 400 gms of rice in his single meal then 100 gms of rice is recommended for these preparations.

The importance of the sequence :

In Manda the proportion of rice & water is 1:14, in yavagu it is 1:6, in vilepi, it is 1:4 & in odana it should be 1:5[4]

For first three meal time 'Mandayukta Yavagu' i.e. a scummy liquid gruel of red rice is advised. Looking at the proportion of water & rice this preparation must be a liquid preparation. This preparation includes liquid food containing solids which are not very difficult to digest.

In 4th, 5th & 6th meal time vilepi i.e. a paste like preparation is advised. In this preparation particle size of the rice becomes very small. Therefore the rate of chemical digestion increases with increased surface area of the food. The mechanical breakdown & mixing with digestive secretions facilities movement of food along the alimentary canal. With little addition of uncting substance like ghee & salt this preparation becomes very delicious & digestive. In modern dietetics such prepartion is adviced to the patients who are convalescing from surgery, gastrointestinal disturbances & acute infection.

In 7th, 8th & 9th meal time odana along with dilute green gram soup, little unction substance & salt is advised. This becomes nutritionally adequate because of the addtion of green gram soup. This preparation is also soft in texture & consistancy, easy to chew & contains low roughage.

In 10th, 11th & 12th meal time odana alongwith dilute birds meat soup with little salt is advised. Birds meat soup is a good source of protiens & after this, patient can switch over to his/her routine diet.

Why Red Rice?

In Samsarjan krama charakacharya has advised to use

red rice for the preparation of Yavagu, odana etc. though it is not available easily every where in the country. The thiamin content of the red rice is more than any other variety of the rice.

Thiamine or vitamin B_1 as it most commonly referred to, is a important member of the B group of vitamins & is the first of the vitamins to be discovered. Thiamine is concerned in proper utilization of carbohydrates in the body and in the absence of adequate amounts of thiamine full utilization of sugars & starches for meeting the energy needs is adversely affected[5].

This amount of thiamine needed by the tissues is directly related to body weight, the metabolic rate & the level of physical activity & depends on the composition of the diet. As the thiamine is specifically employed in carbohydrate utilization the amount required is directly related to the amount of glucose which the diet yeilds. Thiamine is synthesized in unknown & variable amounts by the intestinal bacteria[6].

In the tissue thiamine is found in the phosphorelated form as disphosphothiamine, which is a coenzyme for reactions which involve decarboxylation of acids. Such decarboxylations (The reverse process called co_2 fixation) play an important part in the dissimilation of the metabolites which enter the common metabolic pool[7].

The outer layer of the rice is one of the richest source of the thiamine & removal of the outer bran layer of grain results in removal of thiamine. Therefore polished rice should not be used in sansarjan krama. In absence of red rice, hand poundle unpolished rice is advisable for sansarjan krama.

Unction subsatnce and the salt

Mainly ghee is advised for unction in sansarjan krama. Besides its energy producing property the presence of fat in the diet reduces the need for thiamine & hence fat is said to have thiamine sparing action[8]. Probably this is the reason behind charakacharya's advice to add little unction substance when the rice content increases in sansarjan krama from 4th Annakala.

Salt improves the taste of the food & with little unction substance the prepartion becomes delicious. At the same time salt provides necessary amount of sodium required by the body. A normal sodium concentration is necessary for the correct functioning of all excitable tissues (never skeletal & cardiac muscle) & perhaps of all cells. Green gram that is a good source of potassium which helps to creat balance in the body.

The importance of mudga yush & mansaras yush

The protein content of rice varies from 6-9% depending on the variety. The chief protein is glutelin. Small quantities of albumin, globulin & prolactins are also present. The proteins are limiting in lysine & threonine & to a lesser extent in methionine. The protein effciency ratio of rice protein increases when it is supplimented with lysine, threonine & methionine[9]. These amino acids are found in good quantity in green gram & in the meat of the birds. That is why the green gram soup & birds meat soup is advised along with the rice preparation.

Recent Observations : In a study Panchakarma conducted at S. S. Hospital BHU by R. H. Singh & others, after vaman the patients were given a short course of sansarjan krama. The investigators did not strictly stick to the usual sansarjan krama of Peya, Vilepi, Odana etc. They found a 'Krishra' diet for subsequent 2-3 days as good as any kind of sansarjan krama regime. They found it extremely convenient for the patient as well as for the management[10]. The variety of rice & whether the unction substance like ghee & the salt is used or not is not mentioned in the study. Krishara is a preparation of rice & pulse together & is suppose to be a good source of balanced protein.

Conclusion : From the discussion mentioned above, it is clear that the planning of sansarjan krama is very logical from the modern view point. So while changing the pattern one should be sure that the basic principles does not neglected.

The rice used should not be milled. It should be atleast handpounded. The unction substance like ghee & the salt also have a significant role so these two should be used where it is mentioned. Addition of high protein material like green gram etc. is also essential from nutritional point of view.

References

1) Charak Siddhi 1/12

2) Charak sutra 15/16

3) Sushrut chikitsa 39/8

4) Sushrut sutra 46/344 Dalhan's comment

5) Nutritive value of Indian foods-Page 15, 1995 edition, NIN Hyderabad.

6) Applied physiology, samson wright 13th edition Page 491

7) Applied physiology, samson wright 13th edition Page 492

8) Nutrities value of Indian foods 1995 edition NIN Hyderabad, Page 15

9) Essentials of foods & nutrition Vol 1 Page 717,
By M. Swaminathan. BAPPCO Publications - 1985.

■■■

18. SOME FOOD ARTICLES

1. AMRA (MANGO)

Latin : Mangifera Indica

English : Mango

Rasa (Taste) : Madhur (Sweet) Amla (Sour)

Veerya : (Potency) : Ushna (hot)

Vipaka (Post Digest effect) : Madhur (Sweet)

Properties : Vrushya (Afrodisiac)

Balya (provides strength)

Agni Vardhak (Appetiser)

Useful in Dysentry Vatanashak

2. APPLE

Latin : Pyrus Malus

English : Apple

Rasa (Taste) : Madhur (Sweet)

Veera (Potency) : Sheeta (Cold)

Vipaka (Post digestive effect) : Madhur (Sweet)

Action on Doshas : Alliviates Vata & Pitta, Kapha Aggravates

Properties : Pushtivardha (Anabolic)

: Tasty, Increases Veerya (Sperm Count/Shukra)

3. DRAKSHA

Latin	:	Vitis Vineera
English	:	Grape, Raisins
Rasa (Taste)	:	Madhur (Sweet)
Veerya (Potency)	:	Sheeta (Cold)
Vipaka (Post Digestive effect)	:	Madhur (Sweet)
Properties	:	Netrya (Benificial to eye)
		Pushtikarak (Anabolic)
		Swarya (Useful for Voice)
		Mild Laxative
		Vrushya (Aphrodisiac)
CURES	:	Fever (Jwara)
		Shwasa (Breathellesness)
		Kaša (Cough)
		Vatarakta (gout)
		Kamala (Jaundice)
		Raktapitta (bleeding disorders)
		Kidney Problems
		Muscle Wasting

4. KADALI (Banana)

Latin	:	Musasapientum
English	:	Plantain (Banana)

Rasa (Taste) : Madhur (Sweet)
Veerya (Potency) : Sheeta (Cold)
Vipaka : Madhur (Sweet)
Properties : Grahi (Astrigent)
(Post digestive effect) Pushtikarak (Anabolic)
Improves Taste
Increases Muscle Bulk
Reduce Hunger, Thirst
Useful for Ophthalmic Disorders
Prameha (Diabetes)
Vata Diseases
Tuberculosis

5. MELON

Latin : Cucumimelo
English : Melon
Rasa (Taste) : Madhur (Sweet)
Veerya (Potency) : Sheeta (cold)
Vipaka : Snigdha (Oily), Guru (Heavy)
(Post Digestive effect)
Properties : Alliviates Vata, Pitta
Balya (Provides Strength)
Vrusha (Apphrodisiac)
Mutral (Diuretic)

Koshtha Shodhan

(Digestive tract purifier)

6. NIMBUKA / LEMON

Latin : Lemonum Acidum

English : Lemon

Rasa /Taste : Amla (Sour)

Veerya (Potency) : Ushna (Hot)

Vipaka : Amla (Sour)

(Post Digestive effect)

Properties : Alleviates Vata

Deepana (Appetiser)

Pachana (Digestant)

Reduces Abdominal Pain Improves Taste

Extermly Useful in Conditions Due to

Vitiated Vata

Reduced Agni (Low Digestive Power)

Constipation

Cholera Gastroenteritis)

7. WATERMELON (KALINDA)

Latin : Citrullus Valgarus

English : Water Melon

Rasa (Taste) : Madhura (Sweet)

Veerya (Potency) : Sheeta (Cold), Pakwa (Ripe) is Ushna (Hot)

Vipaka : Guru (Heavy)

(Post Digestive effect)

Properties : Alliviates Pitta

Ripe Watermelon Alliviates Kapha & Vata & Increases Pitta.

Harmful for Vision Veerya Nashak

(decreses reprdocutive tissue)

8. CHANAK /Gram

Latin : Cicer Aretinum

English : Gram/Chick pea

Rasa (Taste) : Kashya (Astringent), Madhura (Sweet).

Veerya (Potency) : Sheeta (Cold)

Vipaka : Katu (Pungent)

(Post Digestive effect)

Action on Doshas : Increase Vata

Alleviates Kapha, Pitta

Properties : Vishtambhi (Constipating),

Cures Blood Disorders,

Antipyretic

Balya (Provides strength

9. MASHA (UDADA)

English : Black gram

Rasa (Taste) : Tikta (Britter)

Veerya (Potency) : Ushna (Hot)

Vipaka : Madhur (Sweet)

(Post Digestive effect)

Action on Doshas : Alleviates Vata
Increases Kapha & Pitta
Improves Taste
Gives satisfaction
(Trupti-Karak)
Balya (Provide Strength)
Viryavardhak (Increases Semen)
Pushtikarak (Anabolic)
Galactoguogue

Useful in : Haemorhoides
Facial Palsy
Vata Roga
Shwasa (Breathlessness)
Duodenal Ulcer.

10. MUDGA (GREEN GRAM)

English : Green Grain

Rasa/Taste : Madhura (Sweet)

Veerya (Potency) : Sheeta (Cold)

Vipaka : Madhura (Sweet)

(Post Digestive effect)

Action on Doshas : Alleviates Pitta

Uses : Usefull For Eyes, Antipyretic

Pathya/useful food for Many Diseases.

11. RICE/SHALIDHANYA

Many Subtypes / Varieties

Latin : Oryza Satine

English : Rice

Rasa/Taste : Kashaya (Astrigent), Madhura (Sweet)

Vipaka : Madhura (Sweet)

(Post Digestive effect)

Properties : Laghu (Light), Snigdha (Oily)

Balya (Provides Strengter)

Vrushya (Aphrodisiac)

Slightly Vitiate Vata, Kapha

Alliviates Pitta

Mutral (Diuretic)

Swarya (Improves Voice)

New Rice - Guru/Heavy

Old Rice - Light

12. TUWARI

Rasa/Taste	:	Madhur (Sweet), Tikta (Bitter)
Veerya/Potency	:	Ushna (hot)
Action on Doshas	:	Alleviates Kapha
Uses	:	Grahi (Astringent)
		Agnivardhak (Appetiser)
		Antidote for poisons
		Usefull in Blood Disorders
		Eczema, Vitiligo Worm Infestation

13. WHEAT (GODHUM)

Latin	:	Triticum Valgari
English	:	Wheat
Rasa/Taste	:	Madhura/Sweet
Veerya/Potency	:	Sheeta (Cold)
Vipaka (Post Digestive effect)	:	Madhura/Sweet
Properties	:	Guru (heavy), Snigdha (oily), Sara (Laxative), Balya (Provides Strength), Alleviates Vata & Pitta Increases Sperm Count (Viryawardhak), Sandhankar (Heals wound/fractures, Nutritive Improves Varna (Skin Colour) Ayushyasthapaka (Maintains Life)

■■■

19. DIET, MIND & YOGA

Dictionary meaning of diet is 'Habitual Food'. Another meaning of it is 'Restricted Selection of Food'. 'Restricted selection of habitual food' will express it in a better way.

Dictionary meaning of Dietetics is 'Study of Diet And Nutrition'. Nutrition means 'Nourishment.' It can be said that 'Dietetics' is a scientific study of restricted selection of habitual food. It indirectly suggests that we must give a specific and systematic thought to our food, which we seldom do.

Diet - One of the Essentialities of life :

Food, clothing and shelter are the dire necessities of life. Broader meaning, 'Food' suggests Nutritious food, clean water and pure air. Unfortunately all these three are, to some extent are contaminated or polluted, especially since last 25 years.

Food, healthy life, nourishing food, moderate but regular physical exercise, sufficient physical and mental rest are very much needful.

Food which is well planned and ideal gives us strength stamina and stability. It creates lustrous skin, sonorus voice, satiety and gaiety. It also gives us mental ability and efficiency. In short it gives us healthier and better life full of physical and mental fitness.

Without food, man will go on walling, weakening, reducing and loosing vigour and vitality. He can subsist for at the most sixty or seventy days and then will die.

Functions of Food - Proper food promotes :

1) Growth : From birth to about twenty five years a person grows to the fullest.

2) Repair : A person is always exposed to diseases, and traumaic injuries. The damage caused by them from time to time is repaired by the defence mechanisn of the body.

3) Maintenance : Body cells are undergoing constantly a process of waer and tear. The destroyed cells are continuously replaced by new born cells. The proper balance between the degeneration and regeneration is maintained by proper diet.

4) Energy Supply : Inumerable biophysical and biochemical processes are going on incessantly in the body. For these continuous supply of energy is required. It is supplied by breaking down of food particles in the process of digestion.

5) Protection : To maintain defensive and preventive mechanism of the body intact various normal function of the cells, tissues and organs of the body are required to be maintained. Proper food maintains normal structure and functions of the body in proper order.

Diet and Mind : Yogic and Ayurvedic aspects. Modern Dietetic consideration is only related to body. But it is a uniqueness of Yogashastra and Ayurved which shows intimate relationship between diet and mind. Both the sciences assert with proofs that diet affects mentality of a human being. Satva (vertue), Raja, (Aggresive desire) and Tama (Ignorant sloth) are the basic qualities of mind. Satva-guna is always strengthening, invigorurating and vitalising. Satvaguna expresses essence, understanding, purity, clarity, compassion and love. Rajoguna implies movement, aggressiveness and extroversion and it operates on a sensual level. Tamoguna manifests ignorance inertia, heaviness and dullness.

Satvaguna is a positive virtue and it strengthens and stabilises mind. Rajoguna and Tamoguna are negative attributes which destabilise and weaken mind. Yet all the three attributes are required of course in a balanced state and having strong control of satvaguna,for a normal functioning of mind. As the final goal of yoga practitioner is elevation and uplifting of mental faculties to attain eternal bliss or moksha he/she should do everything to go on increasing his satvaguna through proper diet and good behaviour. In Bhagvadgeeta Lord Krishna says, " Yoga becomes the destroyer of all woes and sorrows and can be accomplished only by him who is regulated and moderate in diet and recreation, regulated in speech and actions, and regulated in thinking and sleeping too.

Ideal Food For Yoga Practitioners :

Food which are sweet, bland, oily, fresh, natural, nourishing and agreeable is satvik diet and promotes health, longevity, intelligence, happiness, vigour and vitality.

Ideal food-stuff for yoga practioner includes the following items and entities.

1) All nuts and fruits especially having sweet and slightly sour tastes.

2) All kinds of vegetables and edible green leaves.

3)All kinds of pulses.

4) Milk (especially of cow), slightly sour curds, butter milk, butter and ghee.

5) Dates, honey, aand jaggery.

6) Wheat, rice, barly etc.

7) Sprouted pulses and cereals.

Food should be freshly prepared and served. Foods to be avoided by yoga practitioners. Food stuffs which are bitter, much sour, saline or salty, excessively hot or cold, pungent, dry burning or irritating, spicy and much oily and of non-vagetarian variety produce Rajoguna should be avoided. Also food items which are half cooked or burnt, insipid, putrid, stale and polluted and also impure produce tamoguna and therefore must be cast off.

Important Rules And Regulations Related to Diet

1) Eat to live but don't live to eat.

2) Eat food which is beneficial (Hit Bhuk)

3) Eat food in a moderate quantity (Mitabhuk)

4) Don't eat food, properties of which are not known to you. (Ashaka bhuk)

5) Don't eat food in hurry or when you are having disturbed state of mind full of tensions, strains, and emotional outbreaks. Regain peace of mind and then enjoy food with happy hale and hearty mood.

6) Wash your hands, feet and mouth, using clean utensils in a clean place which is well lighted and well-ventilated.

7) Fill half quantity of stomach with food, one fourth quantity with water and liquid substances and keep the remaining one fourth for air.

8) A perosn who takes only one full meal a day is called Yogee (or Yoga - practitioner). He takes light breakfast in

the morning and the healthy and happy life.

9) A person who takes two full meals in a day is called 'Bhogi" i.e. a lusty and greedy person who lives mostly to eat and suffers from illness and or illhealth from time to time.

10) A person who takes full meals more than two times is called Rogee or a sick person. He is a gluttonous person and lives only to eat. He is always sick and away from health.

11) Don't do yogic excercises immediately after taking food. It is safe to do them three hours after taking food. It is better therefore do Yogic excercise in early morning or in the evening when the stomach is empty.

12) Don't take food immediately after doing yogic exercises but take food one hour after doing them.

13) Don't go to bed immediately after taking supper but two hours after it.

14) According to Ayurveda well balanced diet cosists of food stuffs having six tastes (Rasa) namely Madhura (Sweet), Amla (Sour), Lavaṇa (Salty), Katu (Pungent), Tikta (Bitter) and Kashaya (Astringent).

15) According to modern dietetics well balanced diet means a diet which must have all vitamins, minerals in a required quantity and the quantity of food should be such so as to provide required calories.

16) It is possible to plan food giving due consideration to each of the three concepts (viz. Yogic, Ayurvedic, and Modern) related to dietetics, after doing 'trial and error' type of dietary experiments by each and every individual until coming to a final beneficial conclusion.

■■■

PART THREE

20. FOOD AS MEDICINE

(Treatment of diseases/disorders by food articles)

Contents

1. ANAEMIA (PANDUROGA)

Red blood cells or haemoglobin is reduced than normal, the condition is known as Anaemia. PANDUROGA in Ayurdeva. For formation of RBCs and Hb the required material if get less or material is there but no proper formation, or destruction of RBCs in the body or RBCs are thrown out of body due to bleeding (Haemorrhage). These are the reasons of this disease.

Symptoms

No enthusiam in daily work, feeling of tiredness after very little wotk. The work may be of physical in nature or mental nature.

palpitation, fainting are the complaints.

Paleness of inner side of eyelids, tongue, lips one can see it very easily.

Digestion, constipation, headache, lack of concentration, irritability, noise in the ears are various symptoms one can observe it in less or more proportion.

We are getting, iron, vitamin B & C, proteins through ou. food which are necessary for formation of red blood cells and haemoglobin. If we consume following food articles in our regular diet, we will not suffer from anaemia and if at all anemia is there it will be corrected.

1) MOLASSES contains more percentage of iron. Iron is important in building of blood. Molasses is on top for source of iron in naturally occuring substances. The iron in the molasses is absorbed immediately and to maximum extent. Use in diet.

2) SESAMAE OIL contains double iron than liver hence it is to be used in diet.

3) Consume PEANUT for several months and Hb % will increase. Such reports are available.

4) SULTANA, ALMOND, PISTACHEO and CASHEWNUTS contains much of iron. Its daily use is beneficial.

5) FIG and GRAPES are useful in anaemia. Eat several times a day.

6) CABBAGE contains easily assimilable iron. It is useful in anaemia. Peaple lived in Greece without any medicine only with cabbage.

7) ONION is having iron which will assimilate in the body, hence its use is beneficial.

8) SOYABEAN is easily digestible protein hence useful in anaemia. Use twice a day.

9) Emblica officanalis (AMALAKI), LEMON, ORANGE, TOMATO and horse raddish tree fruits (shigru) contains abundant vit. C which is very necessary for absorption of iron in Anaemia, hence use it liberally.

10) If folic acid is less in our food we get anaemia hence eat green vegetables, cereals and liver.

11) Use SPROUTED WHEAT in your daily diet you will not suffer from Anaemia.

12) Liver, eggs, split cereals are useful in Anaemia.

13) Corriander, pot herm, corinda fruit are useful in correction of anaemic condition.

14) Use soup of split beans.

2. ANOREXIA (AGNIMANDYA)

No feeling for eating anything. Sometimes eaten less by a person. It is known as Anorexia. If gastric fire is diminished by some qualites then there is no feeling of hunger and food is not digested properly.

In cases of some fever, diseases of digestive tract, intake of alcohol. Specific choice of eating, children are not fed properly then there is an appearance of Anorexia.

Those who are suffering from Anorexia they are advised to eat ice cream with caution. Ice cream produces Anorexia and there is disturbances in digestion.

1) Use SESAME oil with food. It contains vit. B1 hence is very useful.

2) Lemon juice is is useful in Anorexia. Drink 3-6 times a day 2-4 tea spoons with warm water. It produces more saliva and digestive juices

3) Eat MANGO for feeling of hunger and increase quantity gradually.

4) CASHEW NUT is useful in Anorexia it contains vit. B.

5) COCONUT milk /water is useful.

6) GARLIC is very useful in Anorexia.

7) ONION is also useful in such cases.

8) WHEAT with husk, RICE unpolished, PULSES, PEA NUTS, LIVER, BROWN MEAT contains Thaiamine (B1) vit. It is useful in Anorexia. These substances may be used in diet alternatively.

9) Deficiency of niacin leads to Anorexia. Use PULSES,

PEANUTS, BROWN RICE, WHEAT with husk in diet.

3. ARTHRITIS / JOINT DISORDERS (SANDHIVATA)

When two or more bones come together a joint is formed. If there is pain in small or large joint it is called as Arthritis. There is inflamation to some extent present in the joint

1) HONEY is useful in the condition of Arthritis. Eat it 3-4 times daily.

2) MILK is useful in cases of gouts. (Swelling of small joints).

3) To eat an APPLE is a good remedy for Arthritis and gout. When uric acid is a cause of this condition, apple is useful. Acid in the apple reduces the uric acid intensity.

4) BANANA is useful in Arthritis.

5) FIG is good for muscular Arthritis.

6) GRAPES are useful in painful joint condition.

7) AMALAKI (Emblica officinalis) is useful in many diseases of the joints.

8) LEMON is useful in Arthritis and gout. Plenty of Lemon juice prevents saturation and accumulation of uric acid around the joints. That is why there is no repeated attacks of joint pain. It also prevents formation of crystals or stones in the body.

9) ROCK MELON is useful in gout cases.

10) CARROT expels uric acid out of the body from blood hence it is useful in arthritis.

11) GARLIC is useful in gout.

12) POTATO is useful in small joint diseases. It helps to throw out uric acid from the body.

13) FRUITS, VEGETABLES, GRAINS, CHEESE, MUTTON, YOGHURT are useful for preventing the diseases of the joints.

4. CANCER

Cancer was not known in ancient times. This is a disease of modern times. Deficient diet is one of the main causes of cancer which has been established by research. Hence sufficient food must be taken every day. The articles must be manufactured in good soil and the same must be eaten. If quality of soil is not good then crops obtained from such soil are also of inferior quality. There is no cancer till this date in areas of Himalaya, Africa and Brazil.

Preventive measures

1) Eat plenty of MILK, EGGS, FISH, MUTTON - lamb, CHEESE to keep away cancer from you.

2) Use YOGHURT, sprouted WHEAT, YEAST in your diet for getting plenty of calcium and vitamins for keeping cancer away.

3) For preventing one self from Cancer eat 4 spoons of Emblica officinalis (AMLAKI) and equal quantity of honey.

4) 1 tea spoonful of CHYAVANPRASHA (Raktawardhak) be eaten every day. It is a good protector.

Rasanik (4 globules 3 times a day) or 1 tablet3 times a day - good preventive.

Curative measures

There is tremendus increase of white blood cells in Leukemia. Eat ONION abundantly which decreases the no. of W.B.C.S.

ALMONDS are useful in treatment of cancer. One must eat it.

5. CONSTIPATION (MALAVRODHA)

Constipation means no proper / clear bowel action regularly. Difficulty in evacuation. Large intestine becomes sluggish. Irregular bowel habits. Irregular meals, to eat hurridly, faulty food habits are the causes of constipation. Worries, mental strain, fear, sedentary life are the causes of this disease. Purgatives and laxatives are harmful to the intestine.

1) HONEY is mild laxative. Without any trouble it clears the bowels. Due to its sweet taste children can eat very easily. It is useful for patients of any age and sex. 2-4 tea spoons 2-4 times/day.

2) MILK is best remedy for constipation. Due to regular habit of milk drinking there will not be constipation at all.

3) SESAME SEEDS are useful in constipation. It may be used in food. (2-3 times per day).

4) APPLE is good known laxative. It is more useful when taken on empty stomach. (1-3 apples a day).

5) Well riped BANANA is mild laxative and it is useful (1-3 per day).

6) Eat two CUCUMBERS for clean bowel action every day.

7) DATES are useful in constipation. Eat 5-10 dates a day.

8) FIG eating is good. Without straining bowels are cleared. Fig syrup is also used. Eat 2-4 figs a day.

9) GRAPES are good for combating the constipation. It contains acidic substance, which produces more peristaltic movements of the intestine.

10) Fresh GUAVA to be eaten 1-2 a day which are useful.

11) LEMON JUICE 2-4 tea spoons with a cup of warm/ plain water in the morning is a remedy for constipation.

12) Include MANGO in diet whenever possible. It reduces constipation.

13) MUSKMELON is useful in constipation. Eat it.

14) Eat 2 MANDRIN in the morning and at night. Constipation will be cured.

15) RASINS/SULTANAS are known as laxatives. It contains cellulose, which promotes good peristalsis of the intestine.

16) TOMATOS are mild laxatives. Eat riped tomatos. Useful in constipation.

17) COCONUT MILK/WATER is very mild laxative, can be used in constipation.

18) Use in your diet WHEAT with HUSK, BROWN RICE, PULSES, PEANUTS, LIVER, MUTTON it is remedy for constipation.

19) Fruits with skin, steamed vegetables, bread of grains, contains vit. B-1 and hence are useful in constipation.

20) 1 cup of YOGHURT/CURD add 1 tea spoon of sugar, drink it three times a day. It is useful in constipation.

21) 1 glass of BUTTER MILK add 1 tea spoon of sugar and

drink it 2-3 times a day for curing constipation.

22) Eat BEAT every day. There will be no constipation.

23) Eat roasted POTATO every day it cures constipation.

24) Eat RADISH which is useful in constipation.

25) Use BARLEY in diet it is useful in constipation.

26) 1 Tea spoon of GHEE and one cup of WARM MILK at bed time relieves constipation.

27) Masha (Kidney bean) is good remedy.

6. DIABETES

Insulin is formed by the inslets of langerhans in the pancreas and is poured in the blood circulation. It is responsible for maintaining the sugar percentage in the blood at a particular level. Due to some reasons, if insulin is not formed in the body, the blood sugar level increases. This increases in the sugar percentage in the blood is known as diabetes.

Eating is an essential for maintaining the health. But one must eat such food articles which will not increase sugar level in the body.

1) By eating grains there may be sugar in the urine. But it is not the case with the BANANAS. Hence it is useful for diabetic patients.

2) TOMATO contains low sugar hence is good for diabetes.

3) If there is profuse urine then do not eat carrot.

4) POTATO prevents / cures diabetes as per a scientist's view. Eat soup of lentiles.

5) Juice of CABBAGE leaves is effective in diabetes.

6) Snake gourd is good. No calories. Useful in diabetes and for slimming.

7) Gawar (Cluster beans) is useful.

7. DIARRHOEA (ATISAAR)

Loosenes of the bowels. Sometimes peristalsis of the intestine are increased hence one may get loose motions several times a day. Bacteria, viruses etc. enter our body through food, water etc. If there is inflamation of the inner coating of intestine, due to intestinal worms, some drugs, psychological disturbance are the causes of diarrhoea.

1) APPLE contains pectin: It is useful in controlling the loose motions. Children are more benefitted. Give them 1 to 4 teaspoons of pulp of sweet and riped apple. It controls diarrhoea within 2 days. It is also helpful in habit of loose motions. It is controlled. Apple juice is disinfectant for stomach and intestine. It prevents bacterias etc.

2) Raw BANANA is astringent. Mucus membrane of intestine is contracted by intake of this type of banana.

3) GRAPES are also useful.

4) Raw PINEAPPLE is also useful.

5) COCONUT milk/water is also useful in loose motions, Cholera and similar conditions.

6) CARROT is dis-infectant hence useful in controlling the diarrhoea.

7) GARLIC has the same utility.

8) Plenty of WATER is to be drunk for any type of

diarrhoea, it replaces the loss of body fluid.

9) If diarrhoea is due to be deficiency of niacin then one can include peanuts, PULSES, unpolished or brown RICE and WHEAT in his/her diet.

10) Drink BUTTER MILK, TEA and COFFEE.

11) Boiled MILK is useful but raw milk may cause loose motions.

12) BARLEY water, WHEAT, water of white of egg, corn flower, Araroot, Ricewater, Brandy, Sherry are useful in acute diarrhoea.

13) Use BUTTER MILK, Tea, Coffee, Red wine, Wharterbery wine in chronic diarrhoea.

14) Soup of PULSES is useful in any type.

15) POPCORN water and ghee are useful in any type.

16) Eat YOGHURT or curds if diarrhoea is often.

17) Drink MOLASSES and eat sprouted WHEAT.

8. DYSENTERY

It is of two types. Amoebic Dysentery, and Bacilary Dysentery. There is an inflamation of the mucus membrane of large intestine. Only mucus or mucus with blood appears in stools. There ia pain in abdomen, amoeba, bacteria, viruses, chemical substances are the causes of Dysentery.

1) Bacteria of Dysentery are killed in ten hours if HONEY is taken orally. Hence it is useful when one is travelling or eating in the hotel, restaurants, boarding etc. for many days it is advisable to use honey liberally in the diet.

2) Macerate a BANANA, add salt to taste and eat 2-4 times a day for cure of Dysentery.

3) Eat Emblica officanalis (AMLAKI) many times a day or take 50 ml juice 2-4 times a day for curing of blood and mucus in stools.

4) Drink LEMON juice 15 ml tp 30 ml with water 3-4 times a day. It reduces increased peristalsis of intestine and patient gets cured.

5) ROCK MELON is useful in Dysentery hence eat it often.

9. EAR/NOSE/THROAT PROBLEMS

9.1) NOISE IN EARS

It is a personal sensation. It is observed in the diseases of ear and nerves. Excess of some drugs, constant use of telephones, leads to noise in air.

1) Drink one glass of warm MILK 2 times a day.

2) One tablet of AYT at bed time.

3) 4 globules of P in the evening.

4) GC3X : 1/4 tea spoon powder with milk 3 times a day.

9.2) NOSE DISEASES

inflamation of inner linings of the nose, bleeding from nose i.e. epistaxis, are common complaints regarding the nose. Trauma to nose, erosion due to fingers, any foregin body in the nostril, bleeding nose may be observed. In high altitude, in girls or boys at the time of puberty one can see cases of nose bleeding.

1) FIG is very useful in cases of bleeding from nose. Eat it.

2) Soup of CHICK PEAS, LENTIL, RED GRAM are useful in bleeding of nose.

3) POMGRANATE and Emblica officinalis (AMALAKI) are useful in epistaxis.

4) If there is a habit of epistaxis then MILK, BUTTER, GHEE should be used in diet. It is useful.

5) To use cold water for drinking is a good remedy in cases of bleeding from nose.

6) Old BARELY, Horse gram, its soup, Brinjal, garlic, curds, yoghurt and boiled water are useful in many diseases of nose. Use liberally.

9.3) THROAT DISEASES

Sore throat, pain in throat, itching in throat, throat becomes red, inflamed tonsils, painful swollen tonsils are the common complaints related to the throat.

1) Gargle with LEMON juice and water many times a day 2 tea spoons at least 3-4 times a day will giverelief in pain in throat, Tonsillitis, swolen gums, painful gums.

2) Take LEMON juice 2 teaspoons + 1 glass of warm water + 1 teaspoon of sugar and 1/4 teaspoon of common salt to taste,drink it for 2-4 times a day will give relief in Nasopharyngitis with painful throat.

3) In Laryngitis - voice is not clear. In such conditions - eat PINE APPLE, it is useful.

Water vapours may be inhaled for relief.

10. EYE DISEASES (NETRAVIKAR)

Eyes are very important and very delicate organs of the body. Conjunctivitis, vision disturbances are some of the complaints regarding the eyes. Aolochaka Pitta distribances.

1) Use HONEY in your diet for cure of many diseases of eyes.

2) One cannot tolerate severe light (glare) due to deficiency of Vit. A. Use green vegetables, mango, carrot, liver in your diet. It is useful.

3) Emblica officinalis (AMALAKI) is useful for various complaints of eyes. Eat it.

4) MANGO contains plenty of Vit. A. It is useful in eye diseases.

5) CABBAGE contains Vit. A. Hence it is useful in eye diseases and night blindness. Drink 50 to 175 ml juice of cabbage every day.

6) For maintaining good luster (brightness) of the eyes eat milk, eggs, cheese, mutton, oranges, mandrines, green vegetables, carrot etc.

11. EXHAUSTION (Klama)

Extreme weakness or fatigue, tiredness. There are often complaints of tiredness in our everyday life. One cannot perform his/her usual work totally or partly means exhaustion. One cannot tolerate extra physical or mental work.

More work than usual, inadequate food leads to debility, in such conditions glucose is utilised to produce more energy, hence glucose in the blood is reduced. In such cases Molases 4-8 tea spoons and one glass of water to be taken 2-4 times for feeling better. If there is vertigo it is also controlled and one gets enthusiasm.

1) HONEY is easily and instant assimilable food. Honey is useful in physical exhaustion and mental exhaustion.

2) MILK is useful in debility, drink a cup of milk with 2 tea spoon sugar or honey 2-4 tea spoons, 2-4 times a day.

3) SESAME seeds are useful in exhaustion hence eat it after mixing with sugar, or jaggery or prepare sweets by mixing, gram powder, GHEE and SUGAR and eat two times a day.

4) Boil DATES with milk. Drink the milk and eat dates. It is useful in debility.

5) Eat GRAPES. Suggar in it is very easily supplied to all the tissues in the body and produces heat and energy.

6) Eat SULTANA, RESINS for relief from debility.

7) CASHEW NUTS are better combating debility.

8) Use RICE, WHEAT, POTATO, SUGAR, JAGGERY for relief in debility. Carbohydrate in these substances is useful for producing energy.

9) For having vigour and enthusiasm iodine (element) is essential. For getting iodine - eat FISH, FISH LIVER OIL, COCONUT, PINEAPPLE and VEGETABLES grown at seashore.

10) Eat ALMONDS. Useful for reducing exhaustion.

11) PISTACHIO are also useful in such complaints.

12) Masha (Kidney beans), Chanak (grams), Tila (Sesame), Kushmanda, Rice & Wheat are very useful.

12. GROWTH : BODY AND HEIGHT

Growth in size and length of a living being means body growth.

Height and weight is especially more at the time of puberty means for Age 14 to 18 years.

1) Include BUTTER in the every day diet. Height will be more. It contains 80% fat and vit. A & D.

2) BANANA with brown spots on the skin is riped one and best. Give it to children. It is easy for digestion and good for body growth.

3) MANDRINE to be eaten. It is useful in height increasing. 4 tea spoons to 1 cup of orange juice according to age may be given.

4) PEAS are best for growth. It contains superior quality proteins.

5) SOYABEAN or its milk is very useful for body growth.

6) Slow growth of body or less height, it may be due to deficiency of proteins. PULSES, PEANUTS, EGGS, MILK and fish are to be included in diet, for rich supply of proteins.

7) Calcium is necessary for body health and growth. Hence drink milk, pulses, sesame seeds, corriander seeds, fish etc.

8) Drink more WATER. It is useful.

9) RAGI grains(Elucine Coracana) to be given to children for proper and good growth.

13. GYNAECOLOGICAL DISORDERS

(DISEASES OF WOMEN)

1. Menarc means starting of menstrual period in a girl at about 12 to 15 years of age. It is a period of puberty. Girl transforms into a grown woman (menses). There is a develoment of reproductive organs.

If this period is delayed, SESAME SEED are to be included in diet or eaten 1/4 tea spoon with sugar, honey etc. It is useful.

2. Menstrual period occurs normally at 28-30 days. It is discharge of blood through uterus for 3-5 days. If it is delayed CARROT is useful, hence include in the diet.

DRUM STICKS are useful.

RAW PAPAYA is useful. There is a contraction of muscles of uterus and by that helps for regular menstrual cycle.

RAW PINEAPPLE is also useful.

3. If foetus expels out before completion of seven months it is known as miscarriage. It may due to endometritis, Nephritis, displacement of uterus, diseases like syphylis gonorrhoea etc. abnormal growth of foetus defects in ovum,sperms, Toximia of pregnancies etc. If there is a habitual abortion or miscarriage then WHEAT OIL, RICE OIL, COTTON SEED OIL, PEA NUT OIL (Sweet oil) etc. are to be included in diet. It is useful.

4. Bleeding per vaginum means Menohegia. Sometimes it is more.

Emblica officinalis (Amalaki) and honey are useful in this conditions.

Use LEMON JUICE it is useful. AL Tablets/Globules three times a day for three cycles.

5. Leukorrhhoea means white discharge through vagina. Sometimes it may be yellowish. It may have some smell. It may be with menstrual cycle or in between menstrual cycle.

FIG is very useful in such condition .

AMALAKI is very useful.

ROCK MELON is good for relief.

6. Sterility may be primary or secondary. There are various causes. It is due to deficiency of vit. E. Wheat germs, wheat oil, cotton seed oil, rice husk, vegetables are to be included in the diet. It is useful, (GPR) two pregnancy tablets 2-3 times a day for 3-6 months.

7. If baby is breastfed and there is no milk or less milk. Then for increasing it, sesame seeds are useful.

Barley, wheat, mung soup, popcorn, milk, ghee, grapes, bananas, sugar are useful in many diseases of women.

14. HICC UP

While air is entering in the lungs, epiglottis closes the wind wipe and diaphragm contracts and by that air pushes outside of the wind pipe, there is cough and air goes out with pressure and with noise is called as Hicc up.

Indigestion, heavy stomach, inflamation of lower aspect of diaphragm, excess of alcohol, diseases of lungs or brain. Histeria, Influenza are the other causes of hicc up.

1) Drink cold WATER sip by sip till gets relief.

2) Chew ICE which is useful.

3) COCONUT water / milk is useful in this condition.

4) Eat a small piece of JAGGERY. It gives relief in hicc up.

15. HEART DISEASES (HRUDROGA)

Difficulty or obstructions in blood circulation, function of the heart, change in size of heart, inflamation of pericardium or mayocardium, less blood supply to the heart are some of the diseases.

1) HONEY preserves strength of heart. It enhances to some limit. When there is failure of heart, it is very useful. Hence use alongwith Ayurvedic gold preparations.

2) GRAPES are very useful in many conditions of the heart.

3) LEMON reduces the palpitation of the heart. Contraction and relaxation of heart is regularised.

4) MANGO gives strength to the heart muscles.

5) POMGRANATE is best for giving strength to the heart. It is also useful when there is chest pain.

6) COCONUT gives strength, energy to the heart. It contains Vit. B complex.

7) GARLIC is very useful in heart disease.

8) MILK sedates the heart. Reduces complaint of palpitation. Arteries are also cooled, their function is upto the mark. Milk relieves tension on heart and arteries. The whole system is normalised.

9) SNAKE GOURD, green gram (MUNG) soup are useful.

10) Sprouted WHEAT (Vit. E, MILK, yoghurt (calcium), yeast, molasses, curds, brown rice (Vit. B) must be added in the diet.GABBAGE is useful in the condition of palpitation. It reduces palpitation.

11) CARROT leaves juice 50 to 200 ml be drunk for enhancing the power of the heart.

12) Giant Lemon (Matulung) is useful.

16. HEATING / BURNING SENSATION

Sensation of heat in the body. Body temperature is raised instantly then it is known as sunstroke or heat stroke. There is excessive debility, high fever, patient is delerious and becomes unconscious.

1) For burning sensation of body eat CUCUMBER. It has magic effect. It relieves symptoms created due to heat. It contains all necessary constituent though in very little quantity necessary for body.

2) WATER MELON is useful in cases of burning sensation.

3) Eat GRAPES, DATES, POMGRANATES, ROCK MELON for combating the complaints.

4) COCONUT milk / water, Barely / grain water are useful in hot condition of body.

5) Use in your diet MILK, BUTTER, GHEE for relief.

17. HYPERTENSION

It is also known as high blood pressure. when blood is flowing through the arteries or veins there is a natural pressure which is known as blood pressure. (Lateral pressure on the walls of vessels). There is a physiological variation in the normal blood pressure. If high blood pressure persists for long time there are adverse effects on heart, kidney and brain. Hence care should be taken in cases of high blood pressure.

1) LEMON is useful in lowering the high blood pressure. It also reduce discomfort in the abdomen and by that blood pressure too. It also prevents an attack of paralysis. Due to hypertension.

2) One must eat GARLIC every day for lowering and controlling the high blood pressure.

3) MILK, EGGS and all FRUITS are to be used abundantly every day diet. These provides proteins and vitamins for daily use. Avoid oily and fried food articles from the diet. Salt should be minimum in diet. Eat little at a time and divide it into 5-6 times a day. To eat more at a time gives some trouble only.

4) Include BEAT in a diet. It reduces the high blood pressure. Eat leaves of RADISH. Drink juice of radish. It helps in reducing blood pressure.

5) Eat BARLEY. It is useful in hypertension.

6) 100 ml of juice of raw CABBAGE with 1/4 tea spoon of cumin seed powder to be taken in the morning on empty stomach. Take it for two months.

Avoid common salt, yoghurt, meat, fish, frozen food articles e.g. custords, ice creams, jelly, cold water (from refrigerator)

Avoid fatty substances.

18. INDIGESTION

Also known as Dyspepsia. No proper digestion of food then it is known as indigestion. This is not a disease. It is a symptom one can see in many diseases. Errors and irregularities in eating and drinking causes Dyspepsia e.g. to eat on and off, to eat more than required due to habit, to eat hurriedly etc.

Feeling heaviness in abdomen, pain in abdomen, nausea, vomitting, headache are symptoms in Dyspepsia.

1) Take 2 teaspoons of HONEY 3-4 times a day, as honey does not ferment. It is very useful in indigestion.

2) BANANA is best food. If indigestion is due to carbohydrets eat banana 1-3 times a day, as per your taste. It will be useful for you.

3) GRAPES are light for digestion. Hence can be used liberally. Those having delicate digestion - eat 2-4 times a day.

4) Use LEMON juice 2-4 times a day before or after food. It produces more saliva in mouth and stomach (i.e. gastric juice). Hence good for digestion.

5) Take ORANGE juice for curing indigestion. It produces more digestive juices.

6) PINAPPLE is good for digestion. Eat after food. it get rid complaints of digestion.

7) When nothing is digested then take POMGRANATE. It is easy for digestion.

8) Drink COCONUT WATER (milk) for gases in stomach. Take a glass of it three hours after taking food.

9) GARLIC is useful in gases in stomach, discomfort in abdomen.

19. LIVER DISEASES/DISORDERS

Inflamation of the liver, obstruction of bile duct due to stones, worms etc. Atrophy of the liver, nodes on the liver are increase in the size of the liver. These are some of the diseases of liver. If there is an inflamation of the liver and especially of the bile duct the bile cannot flow further into the duodenum and it is absorbed in the liver capillaries and circulates in the blood, the condition is known as Hepatitis.

1) In any disease of the liver, energy of the body is to be maintained which is important. And this function is carried out well by HONEY. 2-4 tea spoons 3-4 times a day.

2) APPLE is useful in diseases of liver and in hepatitis.

3) Enlargement of liver is reduced by FIGS.

4) EMBLICA officinalis (Amalaki) is useful in hepatitis.

5) LEMON juice produces more digestive juices in the small intestine, hence it is useful in hepatitis. There is less / no bile in the intestine for digestion due to inflamation of the liver, hence lemon juice is useful. Lemon juice is also useful in bile stones in the gall gladder or in the bile duct.

6) MANGO is useful in liver diseases.

7) To reduce stones in gall bladder ROCK MELON / MUSK MELON is useful.

8) Raw PAPAYA is best in liver ailments.

9) To eat CARROT is advised in the bile stone condition.

10) Drink MILK, liver will be tranquil. It is useful in liver diseases.

11) Soup of grains is useful (Moog, (green gram), Masoor (Lentil), Toor (Red gram)).

12) Juice of CABBAGE is useful in hepatitis, especially in cirrhosis of liver, of obstructive jaundice.

13) CARROT leave juice is useful in maintaining the strength of liver. Drink 50-200 ml a day.

20. LONG LIFE - LONGITIVITY (DEERGHAYU)

Span from moment of birth to the last breath till death is known as life. Long life means this period is more. During this period there is constant wear and tear, growth of body, reproduction, to adjust according to the circumstances all these functions are carried out by the organs tissues and cells of the body during the whole life.

1) Molases contains plenty of Vit. B complex. Hence drink/eat.

2) CURDS, YOGHURTS are useful for obtaining long life. It contains proteins, it is useful to combat the tear and wear of the body. (Bulgarian people use maximum curd / yoghurt in their diet. There are more people having long life than any other country in the world.)

3) HONEY and APPLE juice are best for long life and health.

4) Emblica officinalis (AMALAKI) is useful in maintaining youth and useful for long life. Its juice or fruits as it is may be eaten for best results.

5) TOMATO is useful for lenghtening the life.

6) To maintain long life CASHEW NUTS are useful.

7) COCONUT is useful for long life.

8) Eat fistful PEANUTS / ground nuts every day for long life.

21. LUNG DISEASES

Inflamation to the lungs or its coverings, breathlessness or fast respiration due to allergy with substance, pneumonia, tuberculosis, cough, common cold are some of the diseases we come across.

1) In Bronchitis cough is troublesome symptom. GRAPES are useful in this condition. Emblica officinalis (AMALAKI) is also uaseful.

2) If there is haemoptysis in any disease of the lungs, then LEMON juice is a good remedy. Drink 4 teaspoon juice with one glass of water.

3) LEMON is also useful in pneumonia.

4) GARLIC contains a useful volatile oil. If we eat garlic this oil enter in the lungs, hence useful in pneumonia.

5) 1 part garlic and 5 part water drink this mixture for attack of influenza and bronchitis. It gives good relief.

Garlic is also uaseful in Bronchial asthama.

Garlic is a good remedy for cough.

Garlic is also useful in chronic common cold or sinusitis.

Eat pop corns or garlic for cough.

6) Hot water, wine, honey are useful in cough

problems.

7) To increase resistance of lungs drink CARROT leaves juice 50 ml to 200 ml every day.

22. MEMORY (SMRUTI)

Old experience, knowledge, ideas, different sensations, thoughts recorded in Brain centres is known as memory. In some diseases there is a forgetfulness.

1) Sesame seed are useful in this condition. Use in diet.

2) Add in your diet MILK, CHEESE, sprouted WHEAT, YEAST and YOGHURT to combat forgetfulness.

3) RAGI (Nachani) - grains are useful.

23. MENTAL DISEASES/DISORDERS

Functions of mind are very complicated. Mental diseases and body diseases are related to each other hence known as psycocosmatic disesases. Eating or drinking habits, atmosphere around us, non fulfilment of various desires and ambitions are some of the causes of such ailments.

1) SOYABEAN is best for proper growth of the brain and nerves and to maintain its efficiancy.

2) When there is work related to the brain strain, then eat ALMONDS. It It contains vit. Thiamine which is useful.

3) If person is irritable, then keep RASINS / sultanas in water overnight. Macerate in the morning. Filter the water. Add LEMON juice and drink it. It is best remedy for such habit.

4) CASHEW NUTS are best for reducing the exhaustion

of the brain.

5) PISTACHEO NUTS are best in the diseases of nerves.

6) Depression is due to lack of vit. B complex. Brown RICE, WHEAT with HUSK, PULSES, PEA NUTS, LIVER, MUTTON are useful in such cases.

7) If calcium intake is less then there is an irritability. So use MILK, CARROT, FISH, curry leaves in the diet.

8) To maintain the cells in the brain in active state eat liver, brain, kidney, bread, yeast.

9) To reduce nervousness drink FRUIT JUICE, MILK with sugar, Biscuts in between the meals.

10) MILK, CHEESE, sprouted wheat, yeast are useful in forgetfulness.

24. OBESITY (STHOULYA)

More increase in body weight than desired, increase the size of the body is known as obesity.

To eat more, some deformity of ductless glands, diseases of nerves, disturbed metabolism of water and salt are the causes of obesity.

1) There is a obesity due to excessive eating. Drink only MANDRINE juice for 40 days. It is beneficial.

2) GRAPES are good to reduce fattyness of the body.

3) TOMATOS are better for reducing the body weight.

4) Use plenty of VEGETABLES in the diet. It provides vitamins and mineral. Body weight is controlled, there is no feeling of weakness, sensation of fulness of the stomach but there will not be more calories.

5) HONEY is useful in such conditions. 4 teaspoons of honey 3-4 times a day for 2-4 months may be consumed.

6) Triphala guggulu is useful.

25. PARALYSIS/PARESIS (PAKSHAGHAT)

Half side of body if paralysed is known as paralysis of that side. It loses its energy, cannot move it voluntarily i.e. according to our wish as before. Sometimes one arm and forearm, one leg and thigh, both lower extremeties may be affected. Paresis means loss of movement of a part, causes are as follows :- inflamation of brain, an embolus in an artery leading to brain, due to brain haemorrhage and pressure of the blood therein.

1) To prevent atherosclerosis or brittleness of the blood vessels vit. C and calcium are essential. To get this, eat everyday EMBLICA OFFICINALIS, ORANGES, MANDRIN, LEMON, GUAVA. These also contain vit. D in addition.

2) TOMATO and BARELY contains a substance known as Rutin, which is useful in stopping the bleeding hence use it.

3) HONEY is useful in paralysis, Bell's palsy and hemiparesis.

26. PILES

Swelling and forming a small erruption inside or outside the anus is known as piles. Constipation, sedentary habits or profession, constant use of cold or soft chair, liver and blood vessels if diseased due to excess of alcohol are the causes of piles. Pain, itching at the side of anus, Bleeding after evacuation of bowels, are the symptoms. If there is more bleeding, anaemia may ensue.

1) MILK is useful in piles.

2) SESAME SEEDS are useful in this condition, eat it.

3) Emblica officinalis (AMALAKI) is good remedy, eat it.

4) GARLIC is also useful, use it in diet.

5) ONION juice two tea spoons and two tea spoons of sugar, eat 3-4 time a day, it is a good remedy.

6) BARLEY, WHEAT, GRAINS, Brinjal, Snake gourd, vegetables and butter milk, butter, sheep milk are useful in piles hence include in your diet.

27. PYREXIA (FEVER) (JWARA)

Fever or pyrexia means rise in body temperature. When there is increase in body temperature metabolic action is also increased. (Anabolic and katabolic action). Due to this increased metabolic action more carbohydrates, protenis and fluid is expelled out of body. Sodium chloride is also distroyed.

Due to increase in heat in our surroundings. Entry of bacteria in our body, more loss of fluid from our body, inflamation, infection or trauma to brain are various reasons of fever.

1) There is no proper digestion in any fever. In such condition it is necessary without taxing digestive system energy of the body is to be maintained, and in such condition HONEY is very useful.Take honey 3-4 times a day 2-4 spoons at a time. It is more useful in pneumonia and typhoid.

3) There is destruction of proteins in the fever. Hence it is necessary to compensate the loss of proteins and supply all constituents to the body. CANE SUGAR juice is the best.

4) GRAPE SUGAR is very easily assimilable in the blood hence as a food in fever grapes be utilised.

4) ORANGES are good in any fever. Its juice is useful for body nutrition. It is also very easy for digestion and there is no normal digestion in fevers, hence use in fevers.

5) Soak SULTANA (RAISINS) in warm/cold water for twelve hours. Then this water be utilised for drinking in fever cases. It is very useful.

6) Boil the water, then cool it and use for drinking in patients suffering from fever.

7) BUTTER MILK, COCONUT MILK/water and LEMON are useful in fever.

8) Soup of pulses may be given.

28. SKIN DISEASES (TWAKVIKARA)

Whole body is covered by the skin. Extensive area is exposed to the surroundings. Skin diseases are difficult to cure and treat. Sometimes there are chronic diseases. These diseases become obstacles to health and also interferes with the body beauty. Hence person concerned worries, and due to worry / tension skin diseases are aggravated.

1) HONEY is very useful in many skin diseases.

2) FIG is useful. Use plenty for eating.

3) GRAPES are very useful in many diseased conditions of the skin.

4) MANGO is useful for giving good luster of skin or blossoming the skin.

5) MUSK MELON is best in cases of eczema. If one lives on musk melon for 40 day's continuously then this disease gets cured. There are many such examples. Hence it musk melon.

6) SOYABIN is useful in curing fissures on the skin e.g. fissured eczema. Soyabin is good for maintaining the skin health.

7) If skin is of dry type then use OILS, GHEE, PEANUTS in the diet. It relieves such complaints.

8) In this condition eat green VEGETABLES, MANGO, CARROT, LIVER etc. there will be good result.

9) In deficiency of riboflavin skin becomes dry. Use LIVER, MILK, PULSES, GREEN VEGETABLES, in your diet. One gets relief.

10) In deficiancy of niacin there is itching of the skin, and it turns red. For such condition eat PULSES, PEANUTS, BROWN RICE, WHEAT etc.

11) For proper maintenance of skin, GRAINS, PULSES, LIVER and egg to be consumed daily.

There are wrinkles on the skin sometimes. It is due to loss of fluid and salt from the body, exessive sweating, diarrhoea, vomitting are other causes. For relieving such condition drink common salt mixed water sip by sip many times a day.

If eczema or wounds on skin are weeping or with more secretions then do not consume salt.

If skin is dry, rough and with pruritus then to get rid of

this condition eat CABBAGE or Drink 50-175 ml. of juice of Cabbage.

29. STOMATITIS (MUKHAPAKA)

There is an inflamation of tongue (glossitis) and inner lining of mucus membrane of mouth (Stomatitis). Sometimes erruptions on tongue or fissures can be seen. There is burning or hot sensation while eating, swallowing, speaking and sometimes pain. Caries teeth, faulty dentures, heavy smoking, less immunity, some diseases of blood, are the causes.

1) If stomatitis is due to deficiency of riboflavin then MILK, GREEN VEGETABLES, LIVER are useful.

2) BARELY and other cereals are to be used in the form of soup.

3) Leuke warm WATER for drinking is useful.

4) CORRIANDER leaves to be chewed. It helps for relief of this condition.

5) CARROT leaves may be chewed for relief.

6) Roast or bake POTATO and eat it. It is very useful.

7) Fresh PEANUTS are useful in this condition.

30. THIRST (TRUSHNA)

Desire for liquid, or water is known as Thirst. Fever and some other diseases thirst is a symptom in Diabetes there is an excessive thirst. In Diarrhoeas, excessive perspiration, haemorrhage, vomiting, chronic nephritis, gastritis, indigestion, salty foods, there is excessive thirst.

1) LEMON with water, or with tea or as it is may be

taken. Citirc acid in lemon reduces this complaint.

2) MANGO is useful in this condition.

3) COCONUT water is very useful.

4) POPCORN, MUNG, PULSES - their soup is useful.

5) DATES, emblica officinalis, POMGRANATE are useful.

6) CUCUMBER, GRAPES, CORRIANDER are useful.

7) Water of CORRIANDER seeds is useful. Drink sip by sip. Sweet - smelling grass is also useful.

8) Heat GOLD or SILVER, insert in water, drink this water after adding little sugar.

31. URINARY DISEASES

Inflamation of urinary bladder, ureters, kidney or stones in it, there is a complaint of difficulty in urination, haematuria, pain in abdomen or back ache etc. If there is a inflamation or obstruction due to any reason to urinary bladder or adjoining organs, there is a pain during urination.

1) HONEY is useful in obstruction in urination, straining while urination, very little urination and it is often. One to two tea spoon of honey 3-4 times a day.

2) In case of oliguria juice of SUGAR CANE is useful. Drink it 200 ml. 2 times a day. It is also useful in cleaning the urinary system and keep the kidney functioning well.

3) Fresh and raw CUCUMBER is useful for clean and plenty flow of urine.

4) Small urinary stones are reduced / dissolved by FIG. Eat it.

5) Eat GRAPES. Urine will be plenty.

6) AMALAKI (Emblica Officinalis) is useful in burning sensation of urine.

7) Urine flow is also increased.

MUSK MELON / Rock melon are useful for more flow of urine.

8) PINE APPLE is useful for reducing the inflamation of kidney and corrects the functions of kidney.

9) WATER MELON is useful in cases of burning micturation. It also improves the quantity of urine.

10) Coconut milk / water is useful in urinary diseases.

11) Barley, soup of grains, snake gourd, pumpkin gourd, dates, butter milk, Yoghurt and ghee are useful in diseases of urine.

12) APPLE is useful in kidney diseases.

13) Eat BANANAS. Useful in urinary diseases.

14) Eat LEMON or drink lemon juice for relief from haematuria.

15) CARROT produces more urine. Hence it is useful in kidney disease.

16) Eat GARLIC regularly, you will not suffer from urinary stones.

17) MILK is useful for clear urination.

18) Urine becomes acidic in nephritis, cystitis, pylitis. Eat CABBAGE to reduce this acidity. 50 ml to 175 ml. juice of cabbage per day.

19) Drink CARROT leaf juice 50 to 200 ml every day to prevent urinary stones. It is preventive remedy.

20) 30 ml juice of ONION leaves is useful for clear and profuse urine.

21) Eat roasted POTATO it is useful in oliguria.

22) Juice of leaves of RADISH is useful in reducing inflamation of urinary tract.

23) BARLEY is useful in many diseases of urine. It produces more urine.

32. VERTIGO

Sensation of following down or substances around us are in motion or darkness infront of the eyes ia known as vertigo or fainting.

If there is no sufficient heat in the body fainting may occure.

1) Eat RICE, WHEAT, POTATO, SUGAR, JAGGERY, these contains more carbohydrates. You will be relieved.

2) ALMOND may be eaten. It is useful in fainting.

3) MILK, WATER, BANANA, COCONUT, POMGRANATE, PUMPION gourd are useful in this condition, hence one must eat it.

4) POPCORN water, soup of cereals is useful in patients suffering from vertigo.

33. VOMITING

A substance from the stomach if expelled out through mouth is known as vomiting. Entry of poisonous substances into the stomach, some drugs, in some Fevers, Intestinal worms are the causes of vomiting.

1) In case of persistant vomiting and nothing is retained in the stomach, in such case patient is exhausted, becomes debilitated, then give HONEY 2 spoons 4-8 times a day as it is or with water. Energy / strength of body is retained and increases slowly.

2) Use LEMON. Gastritis will be reduced. Peristalsis of stomach becomes less and by that frequency of vomiting is reduced. Though lemon is acidic in nature it transforms into alkaline substance.

3) MANGO is good remedy for vomiting.

4) Drink COCONUT MILK / WATER for stopping the vomitting. It is better when other attempts ahve been failed.

5) Eat Ice for controlling the vomiting.

6) Prepare a mixture of LEMON, water and white of egg. Drink it. Good for relief in vomting.

7) Mix one spoon of Brandy, Schampane and sparkling soda and drink it. It stops vomiting.

8) Areated waters are useful.

9) Drink plenty of water sip by sip. It is useful.

Put some common salt on the tongue. It helps to stop the vomiting.

10) Grapes are useful in case of vomiting.

11) Lemon juice 2 spoons and a glass of water this mixture is to be taken for relief in case of vomiting.

12) A cup of milk and 1/2 spoon of soda-bi-carb powder.

34. WEIGHT GAIN

Our body weight should be according to / related to the height of the body. If there is loss of weight, there might be some ailment in the body. People are taking many tonic preparations for gaining the weight. There should be proper nutrition of muscle tissues, smooth working of all organs of the body is essential. To have proper or suitable weight is essential for health and for good appearance also.

1) SUGAR CANE juice contains essential nutrient constituents, hence its use in weight gaining is useful.

2) MILK CREAM contains plenty of fatty substances. It also contains other useful constituents for body growth. Hence it is useful in gaining body weight.

3) MILK is useful for increasing body weight. Take 200 ml milk every half an hour, do not eat anything. Take complete rest. One can gain gain half kg. weight every day by this procedure.

4) EGGS are best for weight gain. Proteins and fats in its are useful for nutrition and growth for different body cells. Hence growth of total body and rise in body weight.

5) FISH is good for nutrition, growth and weight gain of body. Aminoacids contained in it are more useful. Fish is easy for digestion. Fish liver oir contains vit. A & D which is useful.

6) BUTTER is light for digestion and useful in this condition.

7) Take BANANAS and milk daily. It is a complete food.

8) FIGS are useful, eat it.

9) MANGO is best for weight gain. Eat three mangos a day and drink some milk. Mango contains less proteins, Milk contains very little sugar. Hence use together. There is good weight gain and good health within a month. Also add honey in your diet the results will be best.

10) CASHEW NUTS are good for desired weight gain.

11) COCONUT kernel is best for this condition. Oil in it is digested and absorbed upto 99.3%. Qualities of this oil are like that of butter.

12) PEANUTS are good for weight gain. There is also increase in height.

13) GARLIC is strength providing, eat it.

14) POP CORNS are also useful.

15) RICE, WHEAT, POTATO, SUGAR JAGGERY are useful.

16) PULSES and GHEE useful for increasing the weight. Food articles containing it are to be consumed.

■■■

PART FOUR

APPENDIX

Contents

21. AHARA : FOOD CONCEPT IN AYURVEDA : SAMHITA QUOTES

1) Defination :

'Aahaar' is that - what we eat

It includes everything we eat or drink.

Aahar (Diet) is the cause of the very existance, 'Engergy (Bala)' 'Varna' (colour) & 'Oja' (Immunity/Ultimate) purified form of all the Sharir Dhatus, Body tissues) of every living being on this earth.

2) 'Diet' is the cause of the birth, maintenance, & destruction of all forms of life on this earth.

From 'Diet' only we acquire following things - growth (constant growth, unhampered growth = Abhivruddhi), Bala (Energy), Aarogya (Wellbeing - Health) Varna (Colour), Indriyaprasadatwa (proper functioning of the Indriyas (Sense Organs).

(Sushruta Samhita, Sootrasthana 46/3)

3) Aahaar Vaishamya (Improper diet) is the cause of Aswasthya (illnes)

(Sushruta Samhita, Sootrasthana 46/3)

4) From all above statements one can say that ' In short everything depends on Aahaar (diet)

(Charak Samhita, Sootrasthana 27/350)

5) AYURVEDIC CONCEPT OF FORM OF DIET

(Aahaar Swaroompam)

According to Ayurved Body is said to be made up of Panch Mahabhutas (Pentads) & hence the food also needs to be Panchbhautic (Made up of Panmch {five} Mahabhutas) then only food can get digested & be utilised for the growth of Panchamahabhutas (the basic constitutents of body) which in turn results in growth of body.

(Sushruta Samhita, Sootrasthana 46/525)

6) The diet should be made up of all the six rasas Shadarasatmak) i.e. Madhur (Sweet), Amla (Sour), Lavana (Salty), Katu (Hot), Tikta (Bitter), Kashaya (Astringent).

It has also been stated that according to the properties diet again ca n be of 2 types i.e. Guru & Laghu (i.e. Heavy to digest - Guru & Easy (light to digest - Laghu).

(Sushruta Samhita, Sootrasthana 46/525)

7) Aahaar Sampad (Ideal Diet)

The Ideal diet should have following properties :-

1) It should be Balavrudhikar - it should increase the strength of body.

2) It should be tasty/it should be such that it should be liked by the one, who is taking it.

3) It should give energy instataneously / immediately after taking it.

4) It should be Sharirdharak (Body maintanace), It should have the capacity to withhold the body & give its strength & energy to carry on its regular functions.

5) It should satisfy the one taking it (Truptikar).

6) It should Hot, Snigdha (unctuous wet/not dry) when taken.

7) Should be taken in proper quantity.

8) It should not be ' Viruddha' specifically (Virya viruddha) (incompatible)

The food (Diet) with all above properties is said to be Ideal Samyak & The Properties together constitute what is called as " AAHAAR SAMPAD"

The Diet which is of all the properties explained above can only do the functions prescribed to it.

8) FUNCTIONS OF DIET (food)

1) Instantly satisfying (Sadya Prinan)

2) Gives strength/energy (Balakrut)

3) Maintains the body & maintains the functions of the body (Dehadharak)

4) Increases longitivity.

5) Increases the Teja (Fire) , vitality (utsaha), Recollecting Power (smruti-Memory), Oja & Agni,

(Sushruta Samhita, Chikitsasthan 24/68)

9) TYPES OF DIET / Aahaarprakaar

There are four types of Aahaar

i) Peya : that which can be drunk

ii) Leha: that which can be licked

iii) Bhojya : easily chewable e.g. Rice etc.

iv) Bhakshya : Hard food substances which need to be chewed e.g.Sugarcane, Bread

10) Some have given 6 types in addtioon to the four stated above they have given 2 more types

v) Chushya : which should be sucked e.g. Mango.

vi) Charvya : which need to mastication by the teetch, these include very hard food materials e.g. various nuts.

(Sushruta Samhita, Sootrasthana 46/494)

11) Some have stated 8 types / forms of food /Diet. In addtion to the above 6.

vii) Nishpeshyaa : Those which can only be eaten after being grinded into powder ,various pastes etc.

viii) Khadya : food substances like Suger candy etc.

(Ref. Dhanvantari Nighantu : 7/86)

12) According to Swabhava (Nature)- Diet has been classifed into 2 types i.e. Guru (Heavy) Diet & Laghu (Light) diet.

Rain water, Raktashali (Red rice), Sathe Sali (Old rice), Mudga, Eina (black deer) & lava are light / laghu.

Milk, sugarcane, Rice of the vrihi variety, Udid & meat of the animals from Anoop Desh - land with abundant water & plantation (Marshy lands, equatorial Rain forests) are considered to be Guru (Heavy)

(Ref. Ashtang Sangrah, Sootrasthan : 10/45)

13. SAPTA AAHARKALPANA (Seven Concept of Diet)

The following points are important in the making the Diet complete - Giving Health or Improper-giving Rise to various diseases.

1) SWABHAVA - Basic nature / properties of the food

2) SANYOG - Combination of 2 or more food material changes the qualities / properties of food material.

3) SANSKARA - Due to some sanskara like boiling, roasting etc. there is change in the properties of the food.

4) MATRA - Quantity of food we take.

5) DESH - Desh has 2 meanings - the Desh - region where the food is being taken &

Secondly Desh means the area the food is been produced affects the properties of food material

6) KALA - The time when one takes the food.

7) VYAVASTHA - The order in which one takes the food.

(Ref. No. Ashtang Samgruh : Sootrasthan : 10:45)

14) TIME OF TAKING DIET

Proper excretion of urine & Stools, Doshas go to there respective sthanas (Swasthana) (Sites) cleaning of srotasas various systems & indriyas i.e. sense organs lightness of body (feeling of lightness), Belching with in proper smell to it, Proper excretion of ' Apaan vayu' Heart becomes Nirdosha i.e. we feel like eating & drinking.

When all the above signs are present then only one should eat; as this is the proper time for taking the diet.

(Sushruta Uttartantra 64/84)

15) It is said that when the Doshas go to their own respectives places (Swasthana) & the Strotaras (System) become clean then only one should take Food.

(Kashyap Samhita - Khilsthan 5/10)

16) QUANTITY OF FOOD TO BE TAKEN

(Matra of food)

According to digestive capacity of Agni. If Agni is weak then one should take food only once or should take food in less quantity.

(Sushruta Samhita Uttartantra 2/64-65)

17) Food taken once i.e. at one time & gets digested completely & properly that is said to be Matra/ Quantity of food to be taken.

(Ashtang Sangraha, Sootrasthan 10/9)

18) Considering four parts of the Stomach, one should take food such that 2 parts of the Stomach get filled by the food taken, one part to be filled by water or other liquid matter & one part should be kept free for the 'Vayu' / Gas to move

(Ashtang Sangraha, Sootrasthan 8/46)

19) One should take diet in proper quantity. The quantity (Matra) of diet to be taken depends on the digestion capacity (Agni Bal) of the person which varies from person to person & so does the Matra.

(Charak Samhita, Sootrasthan 5/3)

20) The amount of food, which without disturbing the equilibrium of dhatus & doshas of the body gets digested as well as metabolised in proper time is to be regarded as the proper quantity.

(Charak Samhita, Sootrasthan 5/4)

21) The proper quantity of food does depend upon the nature of food articles. If the food article is heavy only three fourth or half of the stomach capacity is to be filled up. Even in the case of light food articles excessive intake is not conducive to the maintenance of the power of digestion & metabolism.

(Charak Samhita, Sootrasthan 5/7)

22) IMPORTANCE OF FOOD TAKEN IN PROPER QUANTITY

Taken in Appropriate quantity, food certainly helps the individual in bringing about strength, complexion happiness & longevity without disturbing the equilibrium of dhatus & doshas of the body.

(Charak Samhita, Sootrasthan 5/8)

23) Indicated Food :-

One should regularly take Shastika (a kind of rice harvested in sixty days), Sali (oryza sativum), Mudga, Rock Salt, Amalaka (emblica officinalis), Rain Water, Ghee, Meat of animals dwelling in arid climate & Honey.

(Charak Samhita, Sootrasthan 5/12)

24) Contradicted Food :

One should not regularly take heavy articles such as 'Vallura' (dried meat), dry vegetables, lotus rhizomes & lotus stalk. One should never take meat of a diseased animal. Moreover, one should not regularly take Kurchika (boiled buttermilk), Kilata (Inspissiated milk, pork, beef, meat of buffalo fish curd, masha, & yavaka.

(Charak Samhita, Sootrasthan 5/10-11)

25) ORDER IN WHICH ONE SHOULD TAKE THE DIET

First, one should eat food of Madhura Rasa (Sweet Taste) for the purpose of Vata Pitta Shamana. Madhura Rasa is helpful for ' Shaman' of 'Vayu' present in the ' Pakwashaya' (Digestive tract) (Intestines)

Then one should take sour & salty substances for they do the function of Agnivardhan (Increase the digestive juices). Lastely one should take food of Katu & Kashaya Rasa for the purpose of Shaman of ' Kapha'

Some state a different opinion - one should take fruits like pomegranate first in the diet. Then one should take the liquid material & then lastly semisolid & solid food.

Some others say that solid food should be taken first in the diet.

(Sushrut Samhita, Sootrasthan 46/460)

26) EIGHT FACTORS DETERMINING THE UTILITY OF FOOD.

The Eight factors which determine the utility or otherwise of various types of food are

1) PRAKRITI - nature of food articles

2) KARANA - method of their processing

3) SAMYOGA - combination

4) RASHI - Quantity

5) DESHA - Habitat

6) KALA - Time

7) UPAYOGASAMSTHA - Rules Governing intake of food.

8) UPAYOKTRU - Wholesomeness to individual who takes it.

(Charak Samhita, Vimansthana 1/21)

27) RULES FOR TAKING FOOD

Healthy individuals as well as patients should observe the following , even while using such of the food articles as are most wholesome by nature; one should eat only that food in proper quantity which is hot, unctuous (Snigdha) & not contradictory in potency & that too, after the digestion of the previous meal, food should be taken in proper place with all the accessories, without talking & laughing with concentration of mind & paying due regard to oneself & not too fast or too slowly.

(Charak Samhita, Vimansthana 1/24)

■■■

22. PRAKRUTI (HUMAN CONSTITUTION)
CHARACTORS OF DOSHAJ PRAKRITIES

(A) According to various organs :

Sr. No.	Aspect to be Exmined	Vataja	Pittaja	Kaphaja
1.	Appearance	dry	Delicate, pleasant	Pleasent, mild and delicate.
2.	Constitution Frame	Tall, thin, poorly built, parts of the body are not well placed.	Medium built, delicate, flabby and soft musculature. Moderate	Well built, strong & stout, well proportionate and impressive body, Thick
3.	Colour (Skin)	Brown, Black or blackish dark or blackish complexion.	Pale-yellow or raddish white, red, yellow Moderate.	Fair-white, pale complexion with luster. Overweight.
4.	Bodyweight	Low.	Moderate.	Overweight.
5.	Skin (Twaca)			
	(a) Feel or Touch	Dry, rough, cool cracked.	Warm, slightly oily, soft and thin, wrinkled.	Soft, thick, oily, cold and wet.
	(b) Smell	--	Foul smelling, specially of axilla, groin, mouth.	--

	(c) Perspiration (Sweating)	Slight.	Profuse.	Slight.
	(d) Loma (hair) (Skin)	Dry, scanty, horny black.	Soft, pinkish, yellowish scanty, Oily	Thick, soft and oily, blackish. Wavy.
	(e) Any special	Prominent veins and tendons.	Black or Pink pigment spots, (Naevae) moles eruptions	--
6.	Hair (Scalp)	Dry, brittle, rough, smoky (dusty), bifurcated hair, scanty, Kinky, Black.	Soft, thin, Sparse, pinkish hair, red tendency of early greying and baldness (Premature grey)	dark-black (Jet black) Thick shining soft silky, abundent Oily, Dense
7.	Forehead	Small (Narrow) (less than 4 finger breadth)	Medium (Average)	Large with out balding (more than 4 finger breadth.
8.	Eyebrow	Dry, scanty, irregular.	Thin, soft, regular bow shaped.	Regular dark-black Thick hair.
9.	Eyes			
	(a) Shape	Round or irregular, unequal.	Small	Big fish shaped.
	(b) Eye Lashes	Dry, rough, scanty, irregular.	Soft, thin, scanty	Long, black & thick

	(c) Sclera	Smokey, dry, rough.	Yellowish, capillaries,	Bluish-white clear luster, watery, conjunctive, redish at the limbus
	(d) Iris	Smokey, lusterless.	Yellowish	Dark black with luster.
	(e) Luster and look	Lusterless, sunken dead look	Luster penetrating	Lusterful-soft and oily look.
	(f) Nature	Unsteady.		Steady, Soft
	(g) Eyelids	Remains partially open during sleep, fast twinkling.	--	Slow movements of eyelids.
10.	Nose	Blunt - short	Medium, delicate sharp.	Big - straight.
11.	Lips	Dry, cracked, blaskish irregular shape splitted	Thin, soft, delicate and reddish-medium shape.	Big-soft-oily properly shaped.
12.	Mouth	Dry, open	Hot and foul smelling, tendency to stomatitis.	Excess-salivation.
13.	Teeth	Dry, rough, blackish short, big, crooked.	Yellowish white, size moderate.	White, lusterful, strong, proportionate-well arranged.
14.	Gums	Blackish gums, emaciated.	Spongy gums, Soft.	Pink gums.
15.	Tongue	Dry, cracked, rough, short.	Red, thin and long.	Pinkish white, slimy and thick.

16.	Chin	Uneven, bifurcated.	Thin-pointed.	Broad, thick.
17.	Chest	Small (narrow).	Medium.	Broad, expansible, well nourished.
18.	Abdomen	Poorly built, small,	Medium.	Bulging, flabby, bulkey.
19.	Arms	Short, ill nourished unsteady.	Medium, flabby	Long, strong and stout, steady.
20.	Palms	Dry, rough, cracked hard	Soft, delicate, reddish, perspired.	Soft, smooth, thick, pinkish, well developed.
21.	Thighs	Hard, developed.	Soft, flabby.	Well developed strong.
22.	Calf muscles	Short, prominent and highly developed.	Soft, flabby.	Well developed, strong.
23.	Soles	Dry, rough uneven, cracked.	Soft, thin, delicate perspiring.	Soft, smooth, even, steady.
24.	Veins & tendons	Prominent, bulging.	Thin.	Hidden, not visible.
25.	Nails	Dry, small, rough fragile, cracked blackish.	Soft, smooth, pink luster.	Big, smooths, oily shining, convex pink-white.
26.	Joints	Prominent, not well placed, unsteady noisy Bony markings well seen.	Loose & soft joints.	Strong, well developed, well covered. Bony marking not seen.

(B) Physiological Activities

1.	Activities	Fast, unsteady, tremors. cramps.	Fast, definite.	Slow and steady, heavy-slow gait.
2.	Pulse (nadi)	Thready, feeble, fast, easily changing moves like a snake.	Moderate, Jumping like a frog.	Slow, broad, steady, moves like a swan.
3.	Voice	Rough, dry, weak, stammering, unclear, splitted, vibrating, shrill.	High pitch, clear, average.	Deep, resonating, pleasant, sweet, commanding.
4.	Speech	Talkative and fast incoherent, exciting.	Fast, smooth, debating impressive speech difficult to conquer, insulting attitude, sharp & cutting.	Slow and steady (Monotonus) pleasant speech, continuous, impressive talk.
5.	Appetite	Frequent, irregular, variable, scanty.	Good, excessive, un-bearable.	Slow but steady.
6.	Thirst	Variable.	Excessive.	Scanty.
7.	Agni	Irregular (Vishama)	Increased (Tikshana)	Depressed (Manda)
8.	Acceptance of Rasa - Taste	Sweet, sour, salty, (saline) hot and oily	Sweet, bitter, astringent, cold.	Astringent, bitter hot spicy, dry.

9.	Kostha (Related to digestion and evacuation)	Krura (Hard)	Mrudu (Soft)	Madhyam (Medium)
10.	Urine	Small quantity, frequent.	Profuse, foul smell.	Normal
11.	Stool	Constipated, dry, hard, small quantity.	Loose (Semi liquid) yellow, large quantity, oily, foul smell.	Thick-oily, Heavy whitish yellow, slow.
12.	Sleep	Disturbed (Interputed) Scanty awakeful-eyes partly open during sleep.	Moderate sleep. Little and sound.	Deep sleep, heavy, prolonged, day time too.
13.	Dreams	Flying in the sky-mountain, Jumping, running, fearful	Lights, stars, fire, electricity, anger, violence, battle.	Cold, pleasant, water, lakes, swimming, romantic ocean, clouds, swan.
14.	Sex			
	(a) Desire	Weak.	Weak.	Intense.
	(b) Libido	Weak.	Limited.	Good.
	(c) Semen	Small quantity.	Scanty medium.	Profuse.
15.	Children	Few	Few	Many
16.	Strength	Weak	Moderate	Strong
17.	Menstruation	Irregular, Dymenorrhoea	Profuse bleeding	Regular

(C) Mental Activities

1.	Adventure	Timid	Adventurous	Adventurous
2.	Likes & Desires	Wandering, irrelevant talk, music, laughter and hot climate.	Scented things, perfumes flowers, decorative & coloured clothing, painting, carrying, delicate work, cold climate.	Scientific, philosophic literature, loves music dance, arts, white and faint, colours, hot climate.
3.	Intellect	Wavering, not well organised.	Brilliant, intelliegent.	Good and steady intelligence
4.	Memory	Weak, grasp easily & forget easily, recent memory good, remote memory poor.	Good, sharp	Good, grasp - slow. Steady & prolonged.
5.	Concentration	Unsteady	Steady	Steady
6.	Knowledge	Poor	Moderate	Learned & perfect
7.	Nature, faith	Non religious, undevoted devoid of truth & kindness, uncultured, quarrel-	Non religious, fanatic undevoted, kind to friends only, good conduct, quarrelsome	Religious, devoted, loves truth & kindness, cultured, calm and quiet, helping steady.

		some on helping nature	helping to those who seek for	
8.	Emotions			
	(a) Anger	Gets quickly angry	Quickly Angry	No quick anger, but if it is long lasting
	(b) Jealousy	Jealous	Jealous	Minimum
	(c) Greed	Greedy	Greedy	Non greedy
	(d) Enemity	+ +	+ +	Non enemity. If at all, is long lasting
	(e) Mood	Chaging	Angry changing	Gentle, Steady mood
9.	Friendship	Unsteady - so no real friends	No friendship due to hot temper	Many friends and long lasting
10.	Wealth Financial status	Poor, spends money quikly & on trifles	Medium (moderate spends on luxurious article	Wealthy (Rich) Money saver, spends on food.
11.	Life span	Less	Medium	Long

23. SEASONS

	Varsha Monsoon	Sharad Autumn	Hemant Early winter	Shishir Late winter	Vasant Spring	Grishma Summer	Pravrut Premonsoon
Sweet	+ All tastes should be mild; avoid strong tastes	+	+ +	+	contrainid-cated	+	+ All foods with strong taste must be avoided
Acid or sour	+	contraindi-cated	+ +	+ -	according to Sushrut contrain-dicated	amalaka pomegra-nate, sour tastes indicated	+
Salt	+	contraindi-cated	+ +	+	contraindi-cated	contraindi-cated	+
Pungent	+	contraindi-cated	+ +	contraindi-cated	+	contraindi-cated	+
Bitter	+	+	+ +	contraindi-cated	+	contraindi-cated	+
Astringent	+	+	+ +	contraindi-cated	+	+	+
Alkalies (Kshar)	contrandi-cated because they	contraindi cated	contraindi cated	contraindi cated	+	contraindi-cated	contraindi-cated

Heavy or light	may liquify and increase Kapha Nutritious light advised	light +	heavy +	heavy +	heavy contraindi-cated	light +	heavy contraindi-cated
Hot or cold	hot advised boiled food	cold-indicated	extremely cold contrai-ndicated			moderately cold indica-ted hot cont-raindicated, should avoid excessive cold to prevent effects on nose & throat	
Oily or dry	moderate neither too oily nor too dry	ghee-indicated oil, animal fat contrain-dicated	too dry foods contraindi-cated oily, fatty indicated	oil-Ghee	sharp and dry-oily contraindi-cated	ghee	oily in moderate amounts
Liquids	less fluids indicated				less fluids indicated	excess of fluids	
Fasting	intermittent				Intermittent		
Cereals	cereals more than one yr. old to be	cereals more than one yr. old rice	New grains can be used (less than one	New rice wheat, jawar, bajri	more than one yr. old rice, wheat	more than one yr. old rice wheat	old rice, wheat, jav

	used rice wheat, ragi jav, bajri jwari, vari kodrava puffed rice popcorn of all cereals	wheat, jawar jav	yr. old)-new rice, wheat, jawar, bajri		jawar, jav vari, kodrava bajari, pop-corns, puffed rice, bajari, rajadan, satu	jawar	
Pulses	mug, tur masur, puffed pulses	mug, tur chana, masur beans	tur, mug chavli, chana matki, udid, til	black gram udid, til green gram	chana, masur, mug hulge math	mug	green gram
Fish and other aquatic animals	from lake indicated from river contraindi-cated	from stream indicated	from well indicated crabs. lobsters tortoise, cel, shells conches	from lake	contraindi-cated. Avoid duck lobster crabs	trom water reservoir or tank indicated	from lake indicated river fish contraindi-cated
Meat	roasted meat soups and various pre-parations with panchakola	from Aoopa region contr-anidicated Jangala meat indicated e.g. deer, goat sheep, rabit chicken,	meat of prasahanup. bileshaya and aquatic anim-als are indi-cated. Sheep goat, deer, buffalo, pig,	same as in Hemant	Anoopa meat contr-aindicated Roasted meat of chicken, cock, goat, rabbit,	goat, chiken jangala meat, pigeon rice with meat and soup	Roasted meat or mutton

		black deer kapinjala, pigion, parrot sparrow, peacock, tittir, lava	snake, fox, mongoos, pigeon, sparrow lava, stroke chatak, cork, peacock can be taken		sharabha deer, black deer, lava and jangal animals. Old rice with soups of lava or vishkir animals		
Milk and milk products	hot diluted milk curds medicated with saindhav and pancha-kola to. Butter milk panchkola to be taken intermittently	butter milk and curds contraindi-cated. Boiled milk with sugar payasam	milk, indicated curds, butter intermittently. Basundi.	same as in Hemant	milk, buttermilk with trikatu Curds-contraindi-cated	Buffallo's milk, basundi, payasam, shrikhand (in small quantity)	same as in Varsha
Fruits	amalaka, lemon, pome-granate. Overripe fruits contr-aindicated	kushmand, dates, grapes kismis, chiku, apple, banana amalaka	graps (black) custard apple banana, apple chiku, kavath i.e. kapitha, jack-fruit, coconut, guava, pomegranate	same as in Hemant	mango, pomegra-amalaka, bakul, temburni betal nut jack Fruit cucumber	cocum, grapes karvand, pomegra-nate, Lemon mango, raw-mango, banana	tamarind, lemon, amalaka, pomegranate

			goose-berry, jardalu, pine-apple, pista, almond walnut cashewnut				
Vegetables	Methi green leafy veget-ables, contra-aindicated	Methi, chakvat, kushmand, Dudhi, snake gaurd, sweet potato, karela, dodaka, ghosale, cucumber, tandulja cabbage, amalki.	snake-gourd, kushmand navalcol, carrot, cabbage, raddish brinjal, sweet potato, dodka, onion, pumpkin drum-stick	same as in Hemant kadu nimb	methi tandulja, drum-stick, brinjal, raddish, karala, snake gourd, nimb kadunimb	palak drumstick, punarnava onion, chakvat, tandulja, brinjal, snake-gourd sweet potato, elephant's foot	same as in Grishma, with onset of Monsoon stop leafy vegetables
Spices	ginger, mustard pepper, thyme, coriander, turmeric panchakola padelavana bidelavana	cardamom, camphor, cloves, kankol spices to be eaten less	all spices to be taken	all spices can be taken	asafoetida, pepper, mustard dalchini, ajmoda (Thyme) all spices can be taken, pickles of mango	cardamom cloves coriander cumin seeds	as in Varsha

	use of spices for soups & cooking. Pills of temerind, pudina, asafoetida and 1/4 part of marking nut juice of lemon, onion, garlic, pudina, ginger mixed with saindhava, asafoetida, spices improving digestive power indicated.						
Feverage	old medicated wines prepared from honey and grapes after food Soups of various types supernatant liquid on curds with sunth	wine prepared from sugarcane -sidhu, -honey strong wine contraindicated, cold-flavoured drinks	wines of moha, whisky, brandy, rum beer	same as in Hemant	weak and diluted wines of grapes, honey, sidhu flowers and other medicated, wines Asav, arishta of dates whiskey,	cold-drinks using rose wala, scented with camphor cold drinks of raw mango falsa, mosha, dales, coconut & jam &	wines prepar- from honey and grapes

	pepper and thyme Pomegranate and amalaka lemon juices & their sarabats asava, arishtha				rum, resines of khadira & numba tree.	squashes of of above fruits. Wines in general to be avoided, diluted sour wines indicated	
Drinking	water boiled upto 1/8th volume. Well water to be used. Water from lake & stream contradicated.	water boiled upto 1/8th volume	water boiled upto 1/4th volume	water boiled upto 1/2 volume	water boiled upto 1/2 -volume medicated with dry ginger, catechu, honey, musta amalki etc.	water boiled upto 1/2 volume medicated with rose camphor must and flowers of jai, jui & parijat-	water boiled upto 1/8 volume and and naturally cooled.
Prepared food items	kadhi, roasted papad, boiled steamed items	payasam kheer	basundi, shrikhand, sheera, khichadi laddu of til	sweet and more oily and fatty hot	java kheer, khakra	sheera, shrikhand, prepared food items of wheat, jawar, rice, popcornflour mixed with sugar & ghee for breakfast	same as in Varsha

Sugar and sugarcane products		indicated sugarcane	indicated	same as in Hemant	jaggery (cold)		
Oils and fats	oil to be used	ghee medicated with bitter medicines, oil and animal fat contraindicated.	oil & animals fat indicated with sour, salty and pungent articles	same as in Hemant	ghee & animal fat contraindicated, Indicated, oil, can be taken	ghee indicated. Oil contraindicated	same as in Varsha

24. COMMON DIETIC CONSTITUENTS AS MENTIONED IN AYURVEDIC TEXTS DHANYA VARGA (SHIMBI)

No.	Name of the material	Rasa	Virya	Vipaka	Properties	Uses
1.	Chanak (Gram)	Kashay, (Astringent)	Sheeta (cooling)	Madhura (sweet)	Ruska, (Dry) Light	Vishtambhi (constipation), Vatakarak, Pittanashak, cures blood disorders diseases due to Kapha dosha & fevers, Baladayak (gives strength) & increases Taste.
2.	Kulatha (Flowered Dolicoses)	Katu (hot)	Uahna (Hot)	Katu (Hot)	Light Ushna (Hot)	Pittakarak, Causes blood disorders, Causes burning sensation (daha), Cures Asthama, Cough, Hiccups, Calculi, Chronic Rhinitis, Stops exessive sweating, Removes extra fats, Cures Fevers, Kills worms, Increases Shukra Dhatu

						(Sperms).
3.	Masha (Kidney been)	Madhur (sweet)	Sheeta (cooling)	Madhura (sweet) (oily)	Heavy, Snigdha	Vatanashak (corrects), Improves taste (Ruchi karak), gives satisfaction (Truptikar), Baladayak (gives energy), Pushtikar (increases weight) helps removal of stool & urine , Galactogogue. Increases fats, cures piles, facial paralysis, Asthama, Pain in abdomen after taking food, Increases semen.
4.	Masur (Lentil)	Madhura (sweet)	Sheet (cooling)	Madhura (sweet)	Light, Ruksha (dry)	Grahi (Anti diarrheal), Increases Vata Dosha, Kapha Pitta nashak, cures blood

						disorders, and fevers.
5.	Mudga (Green Grain)	Madhura (sweet	Sheeta (cooling)	Madhura (sweet)	Ruksha (dry)	Kapha-Pitta shamak (alivates) anti-diarrhoeal, little vatakarak, good for eyes, cures fevers, Sheeta (cooling)
6.	Tila (Sesamum Nigar seeds)	Katu, Tikta Madhur, Kashaya (hot) (bitting) (astringent)	Ushna (hot)	Katu (hot)	Heavy, Snigdha (oily) cold to touch	Baladayak Useful for hairs, good for skin, Increases location. Heas wounds earlier, good for teeth &its diseases, decreases the quantity of urine, Grahi (Antidiarrheal), Vatanashak, Increases appetite (Deepan), Increases memory, Increases sperm count.

DIETIC CONSTITUENTS (SHAKAVARGA) (VEGETABLES)

No.	Name of Constituent	Rasa	Virya	Vipaka	Properties	Uses
1.	Alabu (Langanaria Si Ceracia)	Madhura (Sweat)	Sheeta (Cool)	Madhura (Cool)	Heavy Ununctous	Purgative, Balya, (Provides Strength) Vrushya, Aphrodisiac Shukravardhak, (Increases Semen) anti Amlapitta.
2.	Kakamachi (Solanum Nigrum)	Tikta, Madhur	Unushna Sheet	Madhura	Light Ununctous	Alleviates all the three Doshas, Aphrodisiac, Tonic Purgative, Cures obstinate skin diseases including leprosy.

3.	Kusmanda (Barincasa Hispida)	Madhura	Sheeta	Madhura	Light Slightly Alkaline	Helps Elimination of Urine, Faeces & Alleviates, all the three vitiated Doshas, Balya, Varushya.
4.	Palankya Spinncia oleralia	Madhura	Sheeta	Madhura	Heavy Ununctous	Vatakarak, Purgative, Wholesome for intake when boiled.
5.	Tanduliyaka (Amaranthus)	Madhura	Sheeta	Madhura	Ununctous Heavy	Curative for-Intoxication & Diseasing Useful for patients of Raktapitta.

DIETIC CONSTITUENTS (PHALAVARGA) (FRUITS)

No.	Name of Costituent	Rasa	Virya	Vipaka	Properties	Uses
1.	Amalaki (Emblica Officinalis)	Pancharasa (Alavana) Amlapradhan	Sheeta	Madhura	Tridoshnashak	Rasayan, Good for eyes, Vrushya, Ruchikar, Shrama, Vaman, Adhman, Vibandha, Amlapitta.
2.	Amrataka (spondia pinnata)	Madhura	Sheeta	Madhura	Heavy, Ununctous	Nourishing, strength promoting, refreshing, aggravator of kapha, aphrodisiac, produces vata during digestion.
3.	Bilwa (Aegla marmelos)	Madhura Amla Kashaya	Ushna	Madhura	Unctous Sharp	Diffucult to digest, Aggravator of doshas Producer of foul smelling flatus, Grahi.

4.	Kapittha Fernoia Limonia	Madhur, Kashaya Amla	Sheet	Madhura	Ununctous Laghoo Lekhana	Harmful for voice, antitoxic, bowel binding Aggravator of vata, Alleviates dosas & Toxins.
5.	Mrudvika (vitis vinifera)	Madhura	Sheeta	Madhura	Unctuous	Cures thirst, burning sensations, fever, dyspnoea, Raktapitta, consumption, wasting, udavarta, hoarseness of voice alcoholism, dryness of mouth & cough.

COMMON DIETIC CONSTITUENTS - AS MENTIONED IN AYURVEDIC TEXTS

DHANYA VARGA (SHUKADHANYA)

No.	Name of the material	Rasa	Virya	Vipaka	Properties	Uses
1.	Godhum (Wheat)	Madhura (Sweet)	Sheeta (cooling)	Madhura (Sweet)	Heavy Vaat-Pitta Shamak Snigdha (oily)	Viryavardhak, Baladayak (gives strength) Bandhankarak (helps in healing of fractures), Sara (increases movements) Increases longivity (Jeevaniya), Brumhana (Tissue builder), Varnya (improves complexion), Heals wounds, Tasty (Ruchya), Maintains the Ayu (life) Pathyakarak (maintains health).

2.	Rakta Shali (Red Rice)	Madhura, Kashaya (Sweet) (Astringent)	Sheeta (cooling)	Madhura (Sweet)	Tridosh-Shamak Heavy	Balya (giving Strength Varnya Increases quantity of urine, Improves voice (Swarya), Increases Semen, Increases appetite, Useful in fevers, Trusha (Thirst), Poison, Vrana (wounds) shwasa, (Asthama), kasa (Cough), Daha (Burning Sensation of body), Pushtikar.
3.	Shashtika (Kind of rice)	Madhur (sweet)	Sheeta (cooling)	Madhura (sweet)	Light Snigdha (oily)	Baddha Varchas (help in formation of stools), Grahi, Baladayak, (gives energy), cures, fever, has qualities & uses like Raktashali.

4.	Vrhi	Madhura (Sweet)	Sheeta (cooling)	Madhura (Sweet)	Tridosh Shamak Heavy	Same as Rakta Shali
5.	Yava	Kashaya (Astrigent) Madhur (sweet)	Sheet (cooling)	Madhur (sweet)	Ruksha Heavy Picchil (Sticky)	Lekhana (scrapping) Komal (Mudru), Helpful in Vrana, Increase Agni & Grasping, Power (Medha), Swarya (Improve voice), Balakarak (Give strength & energy), Increase 'Vata' & Mala (Stool), Helpful in throat infections. Skin deseases, Medarogo (obesity) rhintis, Asthma, Cough, Blood disorders, Trusha (Thirst) Lumbago, Joint Sprains.

■■■

25. GLOSSARY

	ENGLISH	BOTANICAL NAME	SANSKRUT / MARATHI	
A.	**FRUITS**			
1.	Apple	Pyrus Malus Syn. Malus Sylvetris	सेबफलम्	सफरचंद
2.	Apricot	Prunus Armeniaca		
3.	Banana	Musa Sapientum	कदली	केळ
4.	Bullocks Heart	Annoha Reticulatus	सुदा	रामफळ
5.	Bread Fruit	Artocorpusinsisa		
6.	Cashew Fruit	Anacardium Occidentale	सोफ्वारा	काजू
7.	Cherries	Prunus Cerasus		
8.	Custard Apple	Annoha Squamosa	सुभा	सीताफळ
9.	Currants	Euphorbiecal		
10.	Dates	Phonenix-dactylifera	पिंडखर्जूर	खजूर
11.	Figs	Ficus Carica	अंजूर	अंजीर
12.	Clustur Fig	Ficus Glomerata	सुदुंबर	उंबर
13.	Grapes	Vitisvenifera Labruseana	द्राक्षा	द्राक्षे
14.	Guava	Psidium Guajava	अमृतफल	पेरु
15.	Jack Fruit	Artocarpus integrifolia	शांदाफल	फणस
16.	Jambul Fruit	Eugenia Jambolina	जंबू	जांभूळ
B.	**CITRUS FRUITS**			
17.	Lime	Citrus Acida Auranitifolia	जांभ	लिंबू
18.	Grape Fruit	Citrum Parodisi		

19.	Pomelo	Citrus decumana	मधुकर्कटी	मधुराम्लफल
20.	Orange	Citrus reticulata	नारंग	संत्रे
21.	Bitter Orange	Citrus Bigaradia	कर्ण	
22.	Sweet Orange	Citrus Senesis	मधुकर्कटिका	मीठा निंबू मोसुंबी
23.	Giant Lemon Citron	Citrus Medica/Bimbti	मातुलुंग	महाळुंग
24.	Loquat	Eriobotrya Japanica		
25.	Mango	Mangiteraindica	आम्र	आंबा
26.	Water Melon	Citrullus Vulgaris	छायाफल	कलींगड
27.	Palmyra or Fanpalm Fruits	Borasus Flabellifer	ताडफळ	शिंदी
28.	Papaya	Carica Papaya		पपई
29.	Passion Fruit	Passiflorn edulis or foetida	मुक्कोपीर	(पॅशनफळ)
30.	Peach	Prunus Persica		पीच
31.	Pear	Pyrus Communis	अमृतफल	देशी नशूपथी
32.	Pear Avacado (Butter Fruit)	Perisica Americana	माखनफळ	
33.	Pineapple	Ananasa Sativa		अननस
34.	Plums	Prunus domestica Americana	(अलूच)	
35.	Pomgranate	Punica Granatum	दाडिमफल्	डाळिंब
36.	Raspberry	Rubus Idaeus		रॉजबेरी
37.	Strawberry	Farigaria Vesca		स्ट्रॉबेरी

38.	Tomato / Love apple	Lycoperiscum esculentum		टोमॅटो
39.	Toddy Palm Fruit (Fish tail palm fruit)	Caryota Urens	कपिला	शिंदीफळ
40.	Wood Apple	Ferona Elphantum	गोपकर्ण	कवठ
41.	Zizyphus	Jajuba	बदरी	बोर

C. VEGETABLES

42.	Agathi	Sesbenia-grandiflora	अगस्त्य	हादगा
43.	Alternauthern Sessilis		होनगानेकी भाजी	
44.	Amaranthus Spinosus			कोटेमाठ
45.	Amarnath or China Spinach		मार्दू	तांदुळजा
46.	Amaranthus Viridus			तंदूलीय
47.	Amaranthus Polygamus			माठ
48.	Bamboo	Bambusa - Tulda or dendrocalamus	वंश	कल्कीपान बांबू
49.	Bamboo Manna		तक्शीर	वंशलोचन
50.	Bathua Leaves White goose foot	Chenopodium album	वास्तुक	बाहुआसाग
51.	Beugalgram Leaves	Ocer arietihum	पुट्समजा	हरभरापान

52.	Bitter Sweet Black night sweet	Salanum vigrum	काकमाची	
53.	Brussel sprout	Brassica Olerasea gerniliera	छोटाबुंडा गोबी	नवलकोंड
54.	Cabbage	Brassica oleraseb capita	बंदगोबी	कोबी
55.	Carrot leaves	Dancus Carota		गाजरपान
56.	Celery	Apium graueolense	मुदी अजमोदा	ओवा
57.	Coriander leaves	Corindrum sativum	कस्तुंबरी	कोथिंबिर
58.	Curry leaves	Murraya koenigii or Bergeria koehgii	कृष्णनिंब गंधेता	कढीलिंब
59.	Drum Stick leaves	Morihga Oleifera or pterygosperma	शोभांजन सान्माका हरीतपत्र	शेवगा शिग्रूपान
60.	Evolvulus Alsondis		विष्णुकांता	शंखपुष्पी
61.	Fenugreek	Trigohella Foenum Graecum	मेथिका	मेथी
62.	Garden Cress or water cress	Lepidum sativum	चंद्रशूर	आळीव/ अहाळीव
63.	Indian Sorrel	Oxalis Corniculata	चांगेरी खट्टीबुरी	
64.	Ipomoea or Swamp Cabbage	Ipomoea raptans	मूषकाणी नारी का साग	

65.	Khesari leaves	Lathyrus Sativa	मसूरपत्र मसूर की साग	
66.	Lettuse	Letuca sativa	कदू	
67.	Mint	Metha arvenis	पुदीना	
68.	Dill leaves	Peucedanum graveolens		शेपू
69.	Red Sorrel (field sorrel)	Rumex Vesicarius or Crspus	अम्लवेतस	चुका
70.	Spinach	Spinacia Olerecea	अपोरिका	पालक
71.	Asparagus Adsiendens		श्वेतमुसळी	सफेदमुसळी
72.	Asparagus Sarmentosus		शतावरी	
73.	Atriplex Mountain Spinach	Crosofolia 0r hortnesis		चंदनबटवा
74.	Boerhaavia Diffusa or repehs	Spreading Hogweed Small caltrops	पुनर्नवा	वसु
75.	Brahami	Centella asiatica or Herpestics monniera	ब्राह्मी	निर्ब्राह्मी
76.	Coleus Armmaticus	Didymocarpus pedicellata	पथ्थरफोडी	
77.	Canna Edulis	Indian short	कामानी	सब्जा
78.	Thick Leaved Lavender or country boaroge	Coleus	पाषाणभेदी	

D) NON LEAFY VEGETABLES

79. Amala or Indian gooseberry	Phyllanthus emblica or Emblica offcinalis	आमलक/धात्री	आवळा
80. Stargoose berry	Phylauthus distinchus	लवणी	
81. Ash Gourd or white gourd melon	Bennicapa hispida		बोहळा
82. Bitter gourd	Momordica charantia	कारवेल्लक	कार्ले
83. Bottle Gourd	Langeria Vulgaris	तिक्ततुंबी	दुधी भोपळा
84. Brinjal Gourd or egg plant	Solanum melongeha	पितफळ कलिरिका	वांगे
85. Broad Beans	Vica faba		काळेवाल
86. Double Beans	Faba vulgaris		
87. Calabush cucumber	Luffa aegyptica	राजकोशातकी	घोसाळी
88. Califlower	Bassica Botrytis		फुलकोबी/ फ्लॉवर
89. Chocho Marrow	Sechium edule	विवापती बैंगन	बैल बैंगन
90. Cluster Beans	Syampsis tetragonoloba		गवारी
91 Cucumber	Cycymins sativus	कर्कटी	खीरा, काकडी
92. French Beans	Phaseolus vulgaris	बडीबाकला	
93. Goa Beans		शिणवी	
94. Kandori	Coccinda indica		कंदोळी

95. Ladies Finger or Okra	Hibiscus es culenthus Abelmoschus esculentus	पाताली तिंदिशा	भेंडी
96. Peas	Pisum sativum	सहिला, वार्तुला	वाटाणा
97. Pumpkin	Cucurbita maxima		तांबडा भोपळा
98. Ridge gourd	Luffa	कोशातळी	दोडका
99. Snake Gourd	Trichosanthes anguina		पडवळ
100. Wild Snake Gourd	Trichosanthes Cucumeriha	जंगली चिंचोंडा	
101. Soyabean	Glycine Soja or max		
102. Sundaki	Slolanum Torum		
103. Sword Beans	Convalia gladita	महाशिंबी	अबपानी शेंग

E. ROOT AND TUBERS

104. Beat root	Beta Vulgaris		बीट
105. Carrot	Daucus Carota		गाजर
106. Colocasia	Colocasia antiquorum	Arvi Kachalu	
107. Onion	Allium Cepa		कांदा
108. Potato	Solanum Tuberosum		बटाटा
109. Radish	Rapbanus	मूलक	मुळा
110. Sweet potato	Ipomoca batatus		रताळे
111. Tapioca	Manihot glaziovii		
112. Turnip	Brassica	शाल्म	
113. Yarn	Amorphophallus Canpanulatus		सुरण

F. NUTS AND OIL SEEDS

114. Almond	Prunus amygdalus	मधुर वाताम	बदाम
115. Brazil Nut	Bertholletia excelisa		

116. Cashew Nut	Anacardium Occidentale		काजू
117. Coconut	Cocos nucifera	सदाफळ	नारळ
118. Chest Nut	Aesculus hippocastanum		छोटा अक्रोड
119. Groundnut or peanut	Arachic hypogaca		भुईमूग
120. Pistachionut	Pistachia vera		पिस्ता
121. Walnut	Fungalus regia		अक्रोड
122. Water chestnut	Trapa bispinosa		शिंगाडा

G. OIL SEEDS

123. Caster seeds	Ricinus Communis	एरंड	एरंड
124. Cotton seed	Gossxpium indicum or herbaccum	कार्पास	रुई
125. Gingelly seeds	sesanum indicum	तिल	तीळ
126. Olive oil	olea europoea		
127. Safflower seeds or parrot seed	Carthamus tinctorium	कुसुंब	करडी
128. Sunflower seeds	Halianthus annus	सूरजमुखी	सूर्यफूल

H. CEREAL OR MILLETS

129. Bajara	Pennisetum typhoidiucum	वार्जरी	बाजरी
130. Barley	Hordeum Vulgeme	जव	
131. Oats	Avena sativa		
132. Jawar or	Sorghum vulgare,		ज्वारी

katfir corn or great millet	Andropogon sorghum		
133. Italian millet	Steria Italica		
134. Maize, corn	Zea maize	यवनाल	मका
135. Ragi	Elucine coracana		नाचणी
136. Rice	Oryza sativa	तंडूल, साळी	तांदूळ
137. Rough chaft, Pricky chaft	Achyranthus aspera	अपामार्ग	आघाडा
138. Wheat	Triticum sativum	गोधूम	गहू

I. PULSES

139. Bengal gram or chick pea	Cicer arietinum	चणक	हरभरा
140. Black gram	Phaseolus radiatus	माखमाष	उडीद
141. Cowgram, Chinese Dolicas	Vinga Cylindrica	राजमाष	कुळीथ
142. Field Bean	Dolichos lablab	शिंबी	वाल
143. Green Gram	Phaseolus mungo	मुद्ग	मूग
144. Horse gram	Dolichos biflorus	कुलत्थ	कुळीथ
145. Keshari Dal	Lathyrus sativa	मटार	वाटाणे
146. Lentil Dal	Lensescelenta		मसूर
147. Red gram, Pigeon Pea	Cajanus indicus	तुवीरक	तूर

J) SPICES

148. Asafoetida	Ferula assafoetida	हिंगू	हिंग
149. Cardamon	Elettaria cadamomum	इलायची	वेलदोडा

150. Chillies	Capsiccum aunum		मिरची
151. Cinamon	Cinamomum zexylanicicum	त्वक्	दालचिनी
152. Clove	Eugenia Caryophyllata	देवकुसुम	लवंग
153. Coriander	Coriandri fructus	धान्यक	धने
154. Cumin	Cumimum cymihym	जीरक	जिरे
155. Garlic	Allium sativum	रसोन	लसूण
156. Ginger	Zingibar officinale	आर्द्रक	आले
157. Mase, Nutmeg	Myristica fragrance	जातिफल जायपत्री	जायफळ
158. Omum, Bishop's weeds	Carum copticum	दीपक यवानी	ओवा
159. Pepper	Piper nigrum	कृष्णमरीच	मिरी
160. Saunf, Fennel Seeds	Foenioulum Vulgare	मधुरीका	बडीशेप
161. Sinopis, Black mustard seeds	Brassica Sinopiodes	राजिका सर्षप	मोहरी
162. Tamarind	Tamrindus indica	अम्लिका	चिंच
163. Turmeric	Curcuma Longa	हरिद्रा	हळद

K) MISCELLANEOUS

164. Areca Nut	Areca Catechu	सुपारिका	सुपारी
165. Arrow root	Marauta arundinasea		
166. Betel Leaves	Piper Betel	तांबूळ	विडा पान
167. Sago	Metroxylon sagu		साबुदाणा

168. Sugar cane	Sacchrum officinarum	इक्षु	ऊख
169. Vinegar		शिरका	
170. Yeast	Cervisi actermeutum		

■■■

PART FIVE

REFERENCES

REFERENCES : THESIS

1. Agte survarna /Ayurvedic concept of Nutirition/ University of Pune/Ph.D. Thesis/1988

2' Bhagwat B.K./Pathya-Apathya vichar in Ayurveda/ University of Pune/Ph.D. Thesis/1986

3. Gadgi D.P. /Study of Aahar/(Sanskrut language) University of Pune/M.D.Thesis /1986.

4. Gadgil D.P./Aahar sevana vidhi in modern times / (sanskrut langauge) University of Pune /Ph.D Thesis/1990

5. Keskar B.S./ Swasthavruttokta Aahar /University of Pune /M.A.Sc./C 1983.

REFERENCES : BOOKS

1) Kulkarni P.H. /Ayurveda for you /sagar prakashan/ 1992

2) Kulkarni P.H./ Ayurveda philosophy/ Ayurveda Education series/1998.

3) Athawale V.B./Healthy life/1980

REFERENCES : JOURNALS/OTHER

1) Deerghayu International Vol. 1 to 14 / 1984 - 1998

2) Institute of Indian Medicine/lecture notes/ Intensive Training programme for Foreign students /1988 to 1993.

■■■